Konkan
Cookbook
Sanjeev Kapoor

Konkan Cookbook

Sanjeev Kapoor

Konkan Cookbook

Sanjeev Kapoor

In association with Alyona Kapoor

Popular Prakashan

Popular Prakashan Pvt Ltd
35-C, Pt. Madan Mohan Malaviya Marg
Tardeo, Mumbai 400 034

© 2005 Sanjeev Kapoor

First Published 2005
First Reprint October 2005

(3964)
ISBN - 81-7991-216-7

Book Design: FourPlus Advertising Pvt Ltd
Photography: Alim Bolar
Food Stylist: Harpal Singh Sokhi

Typeset at FourPlus Advertising Pvt Ltd

Printed at Saurabh Printers Pvt. Ltd.,
A-16, Sector-IV, Noida 201301

And Published by Ramdas Bhatkal for
Popular Prakashan Pvt Ltd
35-C, Pt. Madan Mohan Malaviya Marg,
Tardeo, Mumbai 400 034.

To Harsha, my publisher and friend,
who is as passionate about food as I am.

A c k n o w l e d g e m e n t s

A.I. Kazi
Afsheen Panjwani
Alim Bolar
Anand Bhandiwad
Anil Bhandari
Anupa Das
Brijesh Lohana
Debashish Mukherjee
Deepa and Suhas Awchat
Drs. Meena & Ram Prabhoo
Ganesh Pednekar
Goa Portuguesa
Grain of Salt, Kolkata

Harpal Singh Sokhi
Hotel Vallerina
Jaideep Chaubal
Jijesh Gangadharan
Jyotsna & Mayur Dvivedi
Lata Palekar
Lohana Khaandaan
Madhuri Gawande
Mausam Vora
Milind Sohoni
Mrs. Lata & Capt. K. K. Lohana
Namrata & Sanjiv Bahl
Neelima Acharya

Neena Murdeshwar
Pooja & Rajeev Kapoor
Priti Surve
Pritpal Singh
Rajeev Matta
Rutika Samtani
Shivani Ganesh
Siraj Bolar
Smeeta Bhatkal
Swapna Shinde
Tripta Bhagattjee
Vinayak Gawande

India is a country of diverse cuisines that intermingle ever so harmoniously that if one traverses from the northern tip to the southern, from eastern tip to the western, one comes across a plethora of delectable delicacies that have their similarities and yet are pleasantly different. Being an ardent foodie, I enjoy all of them but the food of the West coast of India - the Konkan region - is one of my top favourites. In recent times, Konkan cuisine has become one of the most popular cuisines well showcased by a number of speciality restaurants that draw appreciative crowds. Though Konkan food is largely synonymous with fish, the variety of vegetarian dishes is equally impressive.

The Konkan area boasts of the spiciest and most delicious recipes of fish and other seafood. Konkani, the language spoken by the locals of this region, has different dialects with varied accents that make this belt unique. Konkan cuisine is as diverse as spoken Konkani. As you traverse the region you will sense the difference not only in the taste of the dishes but also in their names. Like for example a dish that may be called 'Sukha' in the Malvan region will be called 'Sukke' in Mangalore. But both mean a semi dry dish.

My association with Maharashtra and Goa goes back to my childhood when we used to frequent Mumbai (it was known as Bombay then) during our school vacations. Since a very early age I was subjected to the various delicacies of this region. Being an adventurous foodie family we always experimented with different foods and what we got to taste during our trips to Maharashtra down to Goa and further to Mangalore can be described very simply as delicious.

I was particularly taken up with the unique tastes of *kokum* and *triphal* which make the cuisine of this region distinct from the others. As is the case the world over, locally grown crops play a key part in giving the cuisine its identity. Besides *kokum* and *triphal*, coconut too is a major crop and therefore is used generously. Kokum is a sweet-sour fruit whose dried skin is used for adding a gentle sourness to Konkani curries. One of the popular beverages that uses *kokum* to good advantage is the *Solkadhi*. *Triphal*, on the other hand is used extensively

Author

in Goan, Malvani and Mangalorean cooking. When added to fish gravies and pulses, it enhances the flavour of the dish. It can be used both fresh and dried.

A vast variety of red chillies are available in the area with varying degrees of spiciness and colour. Though coconut is abundant in the Konkan, it is groundnut oil that is largely used as a cooking medium. In Karnataka, however, coconut oil is also used to add a special flavour to certain dishes. Of course one has to cultivate a taste to enjoy the flavour of coconut oil. I like it but if you don't you can always give it a miss and use groundnut oil instead.

The recipes given in this book cover the traditional fare of Malvan,

Goa and Mangalore. In keeping with the distinctive type of cuisine in each of these areas we have attempted to capture the flavour of each area through recipes typical of the area. However one must keep in mind that any given recipe differs from one household to other since they add their own special touch. Prawn *Ghassi* for example - I have eaten it several times at the Nadkarni's - our family friends - place and enjoyed it thoroughly. Mrs. Kamath, my wife Alyona's aunt, makes it a little differently but nevertheless it tastes simply yummy. And when I replicated it at home, I added my own special touch to it and the result was equally good. I do not know which one is the authentic one. In fact I firmly believe that you should not bind yourselves to any boundaries or limits of what is authentic and what is not. Let your taste buds lead you, and believe me the results will be great.

What distinguishes Malvani fish curries is not just the variety of gravies but also the variety of recipes for the same kind of fish made by a dazzling permutation and combination of spices and ingredients and dry-to-wet cooking styles. The most amazing and fiery pomfret

s Note

curry I have ever eaten is the *Malvani Masala* Pomfret, Mrs. Samant's speciality. The speciality of Malvani food is the punch in it, which is just one of the reasons you will go back for a second helping.

Goans traditionally use a lot of vinegar or toddy (Boy, does it stink!) in their spicy dishes. Toddy is a locally brewed palm vinegar. Garlic is another favourite. Goans believe in preparing everything freshly from raw ingredients, they believe it tastes much better that way. While that may be debated in some circles, one cannot dispute the outcome is usually mouth watering! In fact I personally believe that the Goans make the best crab preparations. I have yet to taste a Crab *Masala* which is anywhere near to the one that Mrs. Mangaonkar makes - it is simply magical. Being a former Portuguese colony, Goan cuisine encompasses Portuguese dishes but is also characterized by strong flavours and tropical notes such as lots of coconut. It also makes exuberant use of many new ingredients such as cashewnuts that first entered India through the port of Goa. The long period of Portuguese rule, besides that of the Muslim and Hindu kingdoms, has left an indelible influence on the original

style of Goan cooking and this has led to an exotic mix of truly tasty and spicy cuisine.

Mangalorean cooking is unique in the way the spices are used to enhance the taste and the flavour. When fresh coconut, chillies and various combinations of spices are ground the result can be described with only one word - culinary magic! The people of this region are fond of variety and therefore have perfected the art of improvising and coming out with a veritable repertoire of perfectly cooked food. Another community that has now adopted Karnataka are the Saraswat Brahmins. Having coursed through various lands the Saraswats have a unique cuisine. They make use of practically every vegetable so much so that even the skins and seeds of many vegetables that most others discard, are used effectively in different *chutneys*. Even fresh fruits like mangoes and jackfruit are used in a variety of dishes both sweet and savoury. Among their vast repertoire *Batata Humman* and Fruit *Sasam* are my all time favourites. Specially the Fruit *Sasam* - I simply love the way Mrs. Hattangadi prepares it - just the right touch of ground mustard.

The Konkan coast running from Maharashtra through Goa down to Karnataka is Nature's paradise. Incredible beachside hideaways, where the only sounds are those of palm leaves and waves on the silver sands, add value to the delectable cuisine of this area. It's a pleasure going fishing in these serene and clear waters. Which is what I did while working on this book as is evident from its cover! The oar that I am holding is a progressive development of the original simple wooden one. Both are equally functional but different in looks. My collection of keepsake recipes from the Konkan region is just that, maybe slightly different from what you know as authentic, but certainly simply mouth-watering for you to enjoy with family and friends!

However, if you cook any of the dishes given here differently, please send us your version at konkan@sanjeevkapoor.com and I will definitely try to reach it out to the numerous food lovers.

All the recipes given herein serve four people keeping in mind that each dish forms part of a menu consisting of complementary dishes.

Happy Cooking!

Measurements

Almonds	10	14 gms	Lemon juice	1 tsp	6 gms
Asafoetida (hing)	1 tsp	4 gms	Mace	2	3 gms
Baking powder	1 tsp	3 gms	Mawa (khoya)	1 cup	180 gms
Bengal gram split (chana dal)	1 cup	208 gms	Medium sized carrot	1	70-75 gms
Black cardamoms	2	1 gm	Medium sized onion	1	85-90 gms
Black gram split (dhuli urad dal)	1 cup	214 gms	Medium sized potato	1	95-100 gms
Black pepper powder	1 tsp	3 gms	Medium sized tomato	1	95-100 gms
Butter	1 tbsp	14 gms	Mustard seeds (rai)	1 tsp	4 gms
Caraway seeds (shahi jeera)	1 tsp	3 gms	Mustard powder	1 tsp	2 gms
Cashewnuts	10	18 gms	Oil	1 tbsp	11 gms
Cashewnut paste	1 cup	228 gms	Peanuts	1 cup	200 gms
Cinnamon	1 inch stick	0.5 gms	Poppy seeds (khus khus)	1 tsp	4 gms
Cloves	10	1 gm		1 tbsp	9 gms
Coconut milk	1 cup	225 ml	Powdered sugar	1 cup	124 gms
Coconut oil	1 tbsp	15 ml	Pigeon pea split (toor dal)	1 cup	205 gms
Coriander powder	1 tsp	2 gms	Red chilli powder (lal mirchi)	1 tsp	3 gms
Coriander seeds (dhania)	1 tbsp	4 gms	Refined flour (maida)	1 cup	116 gms
Cumin powder	1 tsp	3 gms	Rice	1 cup	190 gms
Cumin seeds (jeera)	1 tsp	3 gms	Rice flour	1 cup	140 gms
Egg	1 (small)	50 gms	Salt	1 tsp	7 gms
	1 (big)	60 gms	Semolina	1 cup	178 gms
Fennel seeds (saunf)	1 tsp	3 gms	Sesame seeds (til)	1 tsp	4 gms
	1 tbsp	7 gms		1 tbsp	11 gms
Fenugreek seeds (methi dana)	1 tsp	5 gms	Star anise	2	4 gms
	1 tbsp	11 gms	Sugar	1 tsp	6 gms
Fresh coriander leaves	1 cup	25 gms	Tamarind pulp	1 tsp	7 gms
	1 cup (chopped)	60 gms	Triphal	15	2 gms
Fresh cream	1 cup	235 gms	Toddy	1 cup	225 ml
Garam masala powder	1 tsp	2 gms	Tomato puree	1 tbsp	14 gms
Garlic	10 cloves	13 gms		1 cup	225 gms
Garlic paste	1 tbsp	15 gms	Turmeric powder (haldi)	1 tsp	3 gms
Ghee	1 tbsp	12 gms	Vinegar	1 tbsp	13 gms
Ginger	1 inch piece	7 gms	White pepper powder	1 tsp	3 gms
Ginger paste	1 tbsp	15 gms	Whole wheat flour (atta)	1 cup	137 gms
Gram flour (besan)	1 tbsp	5 gms	Yogurt	1 cup	257 gms
	1 cup	90 gms			
Grated cheese	1 cup	86 gms			
Grated dry coconut	1 cup	83 gms			
Green cardamom powder	1 tsp	2 gms			
Green chillies	10	19 gms			
Green gram split (moong dal)	1 cup	207 gms			
Fresh green peas (shelled)	1 cup	158 gms			
Fresh scraped coconut	1 cup	118 gms			
Honey	1 tbsp	16 gms			
Jaggery	1 tsp	8 gms			
	1 tbsp	21 gms			
	1 cup	205 gms			
Jawari flour	1 cup	112 gms			
Kokum petals	1 cup	112 gms			

CONTENTS

Konkan Cookbook
Sanjeev Kapoor

SNACKS & STARTERS

MAIN COURSE VEGETABLES

MAIN COURSE SEAFOOD

MAIN COURSE CHICKEN & MUTTON

DALS

ACCOMPANIMENTS

SWEETS

Konkan
Cookbook
Sanjeev Kapoor

SNACKS &
STARTERS

Crisp Bombil Fry

(Patya Khalcha Bombil)

Ingredients

8	Bombay duck (*bombil*)
½ cup	Rice flour
½ cup	Semolina (*rava*)
Salt to taste	
½ tsp	Turmeric powder
1 tsp	Ginger paste
1 tsp	Garlic paste
1 tsp	Red chilli powder
Oil to deep fry	

Method

1 Remove the head and the fins of the *bombils*. Cut it from the centre lengthwise and slit it open.
2 Mix together rice flour and semolina and set aside.
3 Rub salt and turmeric powder to slit *bombils* and sandwich them between two layers of cloth and place a heavy weight (like a *paat* - grinding stone) over them for one to one and a half hours, so that excess water from the fish is drained out and absorbed by the cloth.
4 Mix together ginger paste, garlic paste and red chilli powder and apply this to the *bombils*.
5 Heat sufficient oil in a *kadai*. Dust the marinated *bombil* with the rice flour and semolina mixture and deep fry on medium heat till crisp and light golden brown.
6 Drain on an absorbent paper and serve immediately.

Bombay Duck is actually fish typical of the Maharashtra coast.
This fish has soft bones and is eaten along with the bones.

Fish
Croquettes

(Fofos)

Ingredients

500 gms	King fish (*surmai*) (thickly sliced)
Salt to taste	
8	Peppercorns
1 large sized	Potato (boiled & mashed)
3	Eggs
4 cloves	Garlic (finely chopped)
½ inch piece	Ginger (finely chopped)
4	Green chillies (finely chopped)
1 tbsp	Lemon juice
1 medium sized	Onion (finely chopped)
A few sprigs	Fresh coriander leaves (finely chopped)
Breadcrumbs as required	
Oil to shallow fry	

Method

1. Cook fish in one cup of water with salt and peppercorns in a shallow pan till all the water has been absorbed. Remove the skin and debone. Mash using a fork.
2. Mix it with mashed potato, one egg, garlic, ginger, green chillies, lemon juice, onion and coriander leaves. Adjust salt.
3. Divide into twelve equal portions and shape into flat, oval cutlets.
4. Beat the remaining eggs. Dip each cutlet in the beaten eggs, roll in the breadcrumbs.
5. Heat sufficient oil in a frying pan on medium heat and shallow-fry the cutlets till they are evenly golden brown on both sides.
6. Remove and drain on an absorbent paper and serve hot.

Note: You can make these cutlets using prawns too.

Care must be taken while deboning the fish to ensure that no bones are left behind. This typical Portuguese Goan snack is as easy to make as it is tasty.

Spicy Black Pomfret Fry

(Tallela Masalyatla Sarga)

Ingredients

1 large sized	Black pomfret (*sarga*)
1 tbsp	Ginger paste
1 tbsp	Garlic paste
Salt to taste	
2 tsps	Tamarind pulp
2 tsps	Red chilli powder
1 tsp	Turmeric powder
1 tsp	Coriander powder
Oil to shallow fry	
½ cup	Rice flour

Method

1. Remove the scales of the black pomfret and cut it into eight slices.
2. Marinate the fish with ginger paste, garlic paste and salt and let it stand for half an hour preferably in the refrigerator.
3. Mix together tamarind pulp, red chilli powder, turmeric powder and coriander powder.
4. Apply the above mixture to the fish and let it stand for at least ten minutes.
5. Heat oil in a pan. Roll the fish pieces in rice flour and shallow fry in moderately hot oil till done. Drain on an absorbent paper.
6. Serve hot.

A Malvani preparation - it is a spicy and tasty starter.
You can make this dish with white pomfrets also.

Mangalorean Patra

(Patrado)

Ingredients

12 medium sized	Colocassia leaves (*arbi ke patte*)
1 cup	Pigeon pea split (*toor dal*)
½ cup	Rice
1 lemon sized ball	Tamarind (soaked)
10	Red chillies whole (*bedgi*) (roasted)
A pinch	Asafoetida
1 tbsp	Jaggery (grated)
Salt to taste	
Tempering	
2 tbsps	Oil
½ tsp	Mustard seeds

Method

1. Soak *toor dal* and rice together for three to four hours. Drain off all the water.
2. Grind along with tamarind, red chillies, asafoetida into a paste using very little water. The paste should not be too fine.
3. Add grated jaggery and salt to taste and grind again. The paste should be quite thick.
4. Transfer into a bowl, cover and keep aside for three to four hours.
5. Wash the colocassia leaves. Remove the stalks. Thinly slice the centre stem so that the leaves lie flat when placed on the worktop. Wipe them dry.
6. Place a leaf on the worktop, shiny side facing downwards. Apply the paste evenly all over. Place another leaf over it but with its tapering end in the opposite direction of the first one. Apply more paste over this. Similarly use up four leaves per roll.
7. Fold the sides of the leaves inwards and then start rolling into a tight roll holding from the sides. Tie it up with a string. Similarly make rolls with the remaining leaves and the remaining *masala*.
8. Heat water in a steamer. Place the rolls in a shallow vessel and keep it in the steamer. Cover and steam till the leaves turn a lighter shade. This may take fifteen to twenty minutes.
9. Allow the rolls to cool. Remove strings. Cut into one-centimeter thick round slices.
10. Heat oil in a frying pan and add mustard seeds. Once the seeds crackle, place the slices in a single layer in the oil. Shallow fry over medium heat till lightly browned on both the sides.
11. Serve hot.

Note: Alternatively you can deep-fry the *patrado* slices till light brown. Drain and serve hot.

A traditional Saraswat Brahmin preparation, these rolls made with colocassia leaves are a must during the festival of Ganesh Chaturthi.

Steamed Pumpkin Delight

(Dudhi Kadamb)

Ingredients

1 cup	Rice
2 cups	Red pumpkin (grated)
¼ cup	Coconut (scraped)
¼ cup	Jaggery (grated)
Salt to taste	
4	Tender banana leaves or turmeric leaves
4 tsps	Pure *ghee*

Method

1. Wash rice and drain completely. Spread on a cloth and let it dry. When it is completely dry grind to a coarse powder.
2. Mix together rice powder, grated red pumpkin, scraped coconut, jaggery, salt well. Cover and let it stand for about an hour.
3. Divide into eight equal portions.
4. Cut each banana leaf into four pieces or turmeric leaf into two pieces.
5. Wrap each portion of pumpkin mixture in the banana or turmeric leaf and secure with a string.
6. Steam-cook in a steamer till done. This may take fifteen to twenty minutes.
7. Untie and serve hot in the leaf itself drizzled with pure *ghee*.

A light and nutritious snack typical of Saraswat Brahmin cuisine - it makes an ideal breakfast item.

Crisp Pohe

(Kurkuri Pohe)

Ingredients

4 cups	Nylon *poha*
2 tbsps	*Ghee*
1 cup	Coconut (scraped)
3	Green chillies (finely chopped)
½ tsp	Cumin seeds (coarsely powdered)
1 tsp	Coriander seeds (coarsely powdered)
1 tbsp	Sugar
Salt to taste	

Method

1. Heat *ghee* in a *kadai* and gently roast the nylon *poha* over low heat till they turn crisp.
2. Mix together scraped coconut, chopped green chillies, powdered cumin and coriander seeds, sugar and salt well.
3. Add this to the roasted *poha* and toss gently.
4. Serve immediately as the *poha* becomes soggy if left for long.

This snack can be made in a jiffy and is especially handy when there are unexpected guests. Children will love this snack.

Kokum
Sherbet

(Have it chilled)

Ingredients

200 gms	*Kokum*
½ cup + 2 tbsps	Sugar
Salt to taste	
½ tsp	Cumin powder

Method

1. Soak *kokum* in two cups of lukewarm water for ten to fifteen minutes.
2. Mash *kokum* and strain its pulp.
3. Boil sugar, *kokum* pulp, salt and cumin powder for two to three minutes. Add a little water while boiling.
4. Take off the heat, cool the syrup and store in a refrigerator.
5. While serving, put a little *kokum* syrup in a glass. Add cold water as needed, mix well and serve chilled.

A cooling drink - a must serve during hot summer months in the Konkan region. Bottled *kokum sherbet* concentrate is easily available in Lonavala, Mahabaleshwar etc.

Solkadi

(Kokum Kadhi)

Ingredients

20 petals	*Kokum*
1	Coconut (scraped)
6-7 cloves	Garlic (roughly chopped)
3	Green chillies (roughly chopped)
Salt to taste	
¼ medium bunch	Fresh coriander leaves (chopped)

Method

1. Soak *kokum* petals in two cups of hot water for one to two hours. Crush them slightly to get thick pulp and strain.
2. Grind coconut, garlic and green chillies with one and a half cups of water. Strain to get a thick coconut milk.
3. Mix *kokum* extract, coconut milk together to get a creamy pink coloured *solkadi*.
4. Add salt, chopped fresh coriander and mix well.
5. Serve chilled.

Serve it like a drink before the meal. It is generally served with a typical Goan or Malvani meal. It goes down well especially with fish curries.

Solkadi

Kokum
Sherbet

Malvani
Prawn Fry

Stuffed
Pomfret Fry

Goan
Chicken
Cutlets

Malvani Prawn Fry

(The crisper the better)

Ingredients

12 (medium sized)	Prawns (shelled & deveined)
Salt to taste	
1½ tbsps	Lemon juice
¾ tsp	Turmeric powder
3 tsps	Red chilli powder
1½ tsps	Ginger paste
1½ tsps	Garlic paste
Oil to shallow fry	
4 tbsps	Rice flour
4 tbsps	Semolina (*rava*)

Method

1. Wash prawns under running water, drain off excess water and press between the folds of an absorbent cloth to dry. Marinate with salt and lemon juice for fifteen minutes.
2. Mix together turmeric powder, red chilli powder, salt, ginger paste, garlic paste and apply this to the prawns. Keep them covered for thirty minutes preferably in a refrigerator.
3. Heat oil on a flat griddle (*tawa*). Mix rice flour and semolina and spread on a plate. Dust the prawns with this mixture and shallow fry till golden on both sides.
4. Drain on an absorbent paper and serve hot.

A combination of rice flour and semolina (*rava*) give that added crispness which cannot be achieved with wheat flour (*atta*) or refined flour (*maida*).

Goan Chicken Cutlets

(Kombdiche Dangar)

Ingredients

1 cup	Chicken mince
2 medium sized	Potatoes (boiled & mashed)
1 inch piece	Ginger (roughly chopped)
3-4 cloves	Garlic (roughly chopped)
2-3	Green chillies (roughly chopped)
¼ tsp	Turmeric powder
½ tsp	Red chilli powder
1½ tbsps + to shallow fry	Oil
1 medium sized	Onion (finely chopped)
½ tsp	*Garam masala* powder
Salt to taste	
A few sprigs	Fresh coriander leaves (chopped)
¼ cup + as required	Semolina (*rava*)

Method

1. Grind together ginger, garlic, green chillies, turmeric powder and red chilli powder into a paste.
2. Heat one and a half tablespoons of oil in a pan and sauté chicken mince till all the moisture dries up.
3. Mix together sautéed chicken mince, mashed potatoes, chopped onion, ground paste, *garam masala* powder, salt to taste and chopped coriander leaves well. Add one-fourth cup of semolina and mix.
4. Divide into eight equal portions and shape them into cutlets. Keep them in the refrigerator for fifteen to twenty minutes.
5. Heat a little oil on a flat griddle (*tawa*). Roll the cutlets in semolina and shallow fry the cutlets till golden brown on both sides.
6. Drain on an absorbent paper and serve hot.

A tasty preparation, which can be served both as a teatime snack and or as a starter before meals. If made in smaller size it will go very well with cocktails too.

Stuffed Pomfret Fry

(Bharli Paplet)

Ingredients

4 (200 gms each)	Pomfrets
1 tsp	Green chilli paste
2 tsps	Ginger-garlic paste
¼ tsp	Turmeric powder
Salt to taste	
2 tbsps	Lemon juice
As required	Semolina (*rava*)
Oil to shallow fry	
For stuffing	
1 cup	Coconut (scraped)
7-8	Green chillies (chopped)
½ small bunch	Fresh coriander leaves (chopped)
2 inch piece	Ginger (roughly chopped)

Method

1. Wash and clean the pomfrets. Mix together green chilli paste, ginger-garlic paste, turmeric powder, salt and one tablespoon of lemon juice and apply all over the fish and keep aside for half an hour.
2. Make slits on both sides and also give a cut on the top to create a pocket for the stuffing.
3. Grind scraped coconut, green chillies, coriander leaves and ginger into a fine *chutney*. Add remaining lemon juice and salt to taste and mix well.
4. Stuff some *chutney* into the pockets of each fish and also apply on all sides of the fish.
5. Heat a flat griddle (*tawa*). Roll the fish in semolina (*rava*) and place on the griddle. Dribble a teaspoon of oil and shallow fry the fish on low heat. Cover and cook for two to three minutes.
6. Turn the fish and cook on the other side with another teaspoon of oil till done. Similarly cook all the fish.
7. Serve hot.

A Malvani speciality - the coriander *chutney* gives it that extra zing.

Bangda Fry

(Tallela Bangda)

Ingredients

8 medium sized	Whole mackerels (*bangda*)
Salt to taste	
2 tbsps	Lemon juice
10-12 petals	*Kokum*
3 tsps	Red chilli powder
½ tsp	Turmeric powder
2 tbsps	Ginger paste
2 tbsps	Garlic paste
Oil to shallow fry	
1 cup	Rice powder (coarse)
For garnishing	
A few	Lemon wedges

Method

1. Make a small slit at the stomach and clean the mackerels from inside and wash thoroughly. Make four to five quarter inch deep cuts on both the sides, apply salt and lemon juice. Keep aside for fifteen minutes.
2. Soak *kokum* in half a cup of warm water for fifteen minutes, crush slightly, strain and keep aside.
3. Mix red chilli powder, turmeric powder, ginger paste, garlic paste, *kokum* pulp and salt and marinate mackerels in this paste for half an hour, preferably in the refrigerator.
4. Heat two tablespoons of oil in a frying pan. Roll the fish in rice powder and shallow-fry in small batches, without overcrowding the pan, for two to three minutes.
5. Turn the fish, dribble some more oil and continue to cook on medium heat for two minutes or till the mackerels are light brown and crisp. Drain on an absorbent paper.
6. Serve hot garnished with lemon wedges.

Though fatty foods are considered harmful to health, mackerels, which are an oily fish, are an exception. They are considered to be more nutritious than other fish and therefore aid good health. They do have a strong and distinctive flavour but they are an all-time favourite of seafood lovers.

Biscuit Puri

(Biscuit Rotti)

Ingredients

2 cups	Fine semolina (*barik rava*)
Salt to taste	
2 tbsps + to deep fry	Oil
1 cup	Coconut (scraped)
1 medium bunch	Fresh coriander leaves (chopped)
3-4	Green chillies (chopped fine)
½ cup	Gram flour (*besan*)

Method

1. Mix *rava* and salt. Heat two tablespoons of oil and add to the flour and mix gently. Add sufficient water and knead into a semi soft dough. Cover with a damp cloth and let it stand for at least two hours.
2. For the filling, mix scraped coconut, chopped coriander leaves, green chillies, gram flour and salt.
3. Knead the dough again and divide into sixteen equal portions. Divide the filling into sixteen equal portions.
4. Grease your palms, spread one portion of the dough into a *puri*. Place a portion of the filling in the center and gather the ends and roll again. Dip in a little flour and roll into a *puri* of three-inch diameter. Similarly prepare other *puris*.
5. Heat sufficient oil in a *kadai* and gently slide in the *puris* one at a time. Deep-fry on medium heat till both sides are golden.
6. Drain on an absorbent paper and serve hot.

A tasty vegetarian teatime snack. For a variation you can also add roasted and coarsely powdered *urad dal* to the stuffing.

Konkan Cookbook
Sanjeev Kapoor

MAIN COURSE
VEGETABLES

Cabbage with Chana Dal

(Kobichi Bhaji)

Ingredients

1 medium sized	Cabbage (shredded)
½ cup	Bengal gram split (*chana dal*)
2 tbsps	Oil
½ tsp	Mustard seeds
A pinch	Asafoetida
1 tsp	Turmeric powder
4-6	Curry leaves
2-3	Green chillies (cut into two)
Salt to taste	
1 tsp	Sugar
2 tbsps	Coconut (scraped)
A few sprigs	Fresh coriander leaves (chopped)

Method

1. Soak *chana dal* in one and a half cups of water for one hour.
2. Heat oil in a *kadai*, add mustard seeds. When they crackle add asafoetida, turmeric powder, curry leaves and green chillies.
3. Add the soaked *chana dal* and sauté with the above tempering. Sprinkle some water, cover and cook till half done.
4. Add the shredded cabbage and mix it well with the *dal.* Add salt, sugar. Cover and let the cabbage cook.
5. Serve garnished with scraped coconut and chopped coriander leaves.

A mildly flavoured and nutritious vegetable dish which will complement any spicy curry. The *chana dal* adds flavour and substance to the otherwise dull cabbage.

Brinjal and Potato Rassa

(Vangi Ani Batata Rassa)

Ingredients

8 small sized	Brinjals (*vangi*)
2 large sized	Potatoes (thick strips)
3 tbsps	Oil
1	Bay leaf
1 inch stick	Cinnamon
1	Black cardamom
1	Star anise
1	Mace
3-4	Peppercorns
1 tsp	Red chilli powder
1 tsp	*Garam masala* powder
2 medium sized	Tomatoes (finely chopped)
1 tbsp	Tamarind pulp
Salt to taste	
For paste	
1 inch piece	Ginger
4-5 cloves	Garlic
½ cup	Onions (browned)
1 tbsp	Poppy seeds (*khuskhus*)(roasted)
¼ tsp	Turmeric powder
1 tbsp	Coriander powder

Method

1. Wash and slit brinjals into four, keeping the stems intact.
2. Grind ginger, garlic, browned onions, poppy seeds, turmeric power and coriander powder into a fine paste.
3. Heat oil in a *kadai.* Add bay leaf, cinnamon, black cardamom, star anise, mace and peppercorns. Sauté.
4. Add ground paste, stir well and sauté till dark brown.
5. Add red chilli powder and *garam masala* powder and stir well. Add chopped tomatoes, stir well and cook till soft.
6. Add potato strips. Stir, cover and cook for two minutes. Add brinjals, stir and add two cups of water. Mix lightly, cover again and cook till the vegetables are done.
7. Remove lid and add tamarind pulp and salt. Stir and simmer for two minutes.
8. Serve hot.

Note: To make browned onions, thinly slice the onions and deep-fry till golden. Drain on an absorbent paper and use as required.

A spicy and tangy Malvani preparation with medium thick gravy, which goes well with *chapatis*.

Tempered Potatoes

(Batata Bhaji)

Ingredients

6-7 medium sized	Potatoes (parboiled & cut into 1 inch cubes)
3 tbsps	Oil
½ tsp	Mustard seeds
1 sprig	Curry leaves
2 tbsps	Black gram split (*dhuli urad dal*)
2	Red chillies whole
1 medium sized	Onion (finely sliced)
¼ tsp	Turmeric powder
Salt to taste	
½ cup	Coconut (scraped)
A few sprigs	Fresh coriander leaves (finely chopped)

Method

1. Heat oil in a *kadai*. Add mustard seeds and let them crackle.
2. Add curry leaves and *urad dal* and sauté till *dal* turns light brown. Break whole red chillies into two or three pieces and add. Stir and add sliced onion and sauté till translucent.
3. Add turmeric powder. Stir well, add potato cubes and salt. Stir well and cook covered for five minutes on low heat till the potatoes are done.
4. Add scraped coconut and stir with a light hand. Remove from heat.
5. Garnish with chopped coriander leaves and serve hot.

A simple yet tasty Mangalorean dish, which can be made at short notice.
Usually served with rice and curry.

Hot and Sour Fried Yam

(Soorna Koot)

Ingredients

500 gms	Yam (*sooran*)
1 tbsp + to deep fry	Oil
10	Red chillies whole
1½ tsps	Mustard seeds
½ tsp	Fenugreek seeds (*methi dana*)
A pinch	Asafoetida
½ tsp	Turmeric powder
1 large lemon-sized ball	Tamarind
Salt to taste	

Method

1. Peel and cut yam into very small cubes. Keep them in salted water for about half an hour. Drain well and dry on an absorbent cloth.
2. Heat sufficient oil in a *kadai* and deep-fry the yam cubes till golden and crisp. Drain onto an absorbent paper and keep aside.
3. Heat one tablespoon of oil in a pan and sauté whole red chillies, mustard seeds, fenugreek seeds, asafoetida and turmeric powder till a nice aroma is given out taking care that the spices do not burn. Grind to a fine paste with tamarind and a little water.
4. Mix the ground *masala* with salt, fried yam. Add three fourth cup of water so that the yam pieces soak properly in the *masala* paste.
5. Let it stand for two to three hours before serving it.

This is a mild pickle, which will last for a few days in the refrigerator.

Cauliflower in Coconut Milk

(Phoolgobhi Sambhari)

Ingredients

1 medium sized	Cauliflower (small florets)
1 lemon sized ball	Tamarind
¾ cup	Coconut (scraped)
4 tbsps	Oil
½ tsp	Cumin seeds
A pinch	Asafoetida
3 medium sized	Onions (finely chopped)
½ tsp	Turmeric powder
1 tsp	Red chilli powder
Salt to taste	
½ tsp	Sugar
1½ tsps	*Pathare Prabhu masala*
12-15	Cashewnuts
¼ cup	Gram flour (*besan*)
A few sprigs	Fresh coriander leaves (chopped)

Method

1. Soak tamarind in one cup of warm water for half an hour, remove the pulp, strain and keep aside.
2. Reserve one tablespoon of scraped coconut for garnishing. Soak the remaining scraped coconut in one and half cups of warm water. Grind and extract milk.
3. Heat oil in a pan, add cumin seeds and when it starts to change colour, add asafoetida and chopped onions. Sauté till onions turn translucent.
4. Add turmeric powder, red chilli powder, salt, sugar, *Pathare Prabhu masala*, cashewnuts and cauliflower florets. Mix well and sauté for two to three minutes.
5. Add one cup of water and bring it to a boil. Reduce heat, cover and simmer for six to eight minutes.
6. Dissolve *besan* in half the quantity of coconut milk. Mix it well to ensure that there are no lumps and add this to the cauliflower mixture.
7. Increase heat and bring to a boil. Continue to cook on medium heat till cauliflower is cooked, stirring occasionally. Stir in the remaining coconut milk.
8. Serve hot, garnished with fresh coriander leaves and the reserved scraped coconut.

Note: For the recipe of *Pathare Prabhu masala* see page no.138

One of the original communities that existed in Mumbai of yore is Pathare Prabhus. Considered to be a well-to-do community with changing times their opulence has decreased considerably but their enthusiasm for elaborate meals continues. *Pathare Prabhu masala* when added to a dish makes it extra special.

Capsicum Kayras

(Simla Mirch Kayras)

Ingredients

5-6 medium sized	Capsicum (1 inch cubes)
2 medium sized	Potatoes (1 inch cubes)
1½ tbsps	Oil
½ tsp	Mustard seeds
a pinch	Asafoetida
½ cup	Peanuts
¼ tsp	Turmeric powder
Salt to taste	
1½ tbsps	Jaggery (grated)
For *masala* paste	
½ cup	Coconut (scraped)
3 tbsps	Sesame seeds
2 tbsps	Bengal gram split (*chana dal*)
2 tbsps	Coriander seeds
¼ tsp	Fenugreek seeds
4-5	Red chillies whole (*bedgi*)
2 tbsps	Tamarind pulp

Method

1. In a pan dry roast the scraped coconut and sesame seeds separately. Keep aside.
2. Heat half a tablespoon of oil in the pan and add *chana dal*, coriander seeds, fenugreek seeds and red chillies and sauté till a nice aroma is given out. Grind this along with roasted coconut, sesame seeds and tamarind pulp to a fine paste with three-fourth cup of water.
3. Heat oil in a pan, add mustard seeds. When they crackle, add asafoetida. Add peanuts and sauté for three to four minutes.
4. Add the potato pieces, turmeric powder, salt and jaggery. Stir, cover and cook on low heat for five minutes. Add capsicum pieces, stir and cook till the vegetables are half done.
5. Add the ground paste, one and a half cups of water and simmer for three to four minutes.
6. Serve hot.

A Saraswat Brahmin delicacy with an unusual sweet and sour taste.
An essential item of a wedding meal.

Chana and Jackfruit Sukke

(Chana Ani Kadgi Sukke)

Ingredients

1 cup	Bengal gram (brown *chana*)
½ kg	Raw jackfruit (*kadgi*)
3 tbsps	Oil
Salt to taste	
½ tsp	Mustard seeds
1 sprig	Curry leaves
A pinch	Asafoetida
1 tbsp	Jaggery (grated)
For paste	
1 tsp	Coriander seeds
½ tsp	Black gram split (*dhuli urad dal*)
¼ tsp	Fenugreek seeds (*methi dana*)
3-4	Red chillies whole
1 cup	Coconut (scraped)
1 tbsp	Tamarind pulp

Method

1. Soak *chana* in three cups of water for three to four hours. Drain.
2. Apply a little oil to your palms and knife and remove skin of jackfruit and cut into two centimeter pieces. Apply salt to it and keep it aside.
3. Steam jackfruit in double boiler for five minutes. Remove from steamer and keep it aside.
4. Pressure cook soaked *chana* in two cups of water for about three whistles or till soft.
5. Heat one teaspoon of oil in a *kadai*. Add coriander seeds, split black gram and fenugreek seeds. Sauté till lightly browned. Add broken red chillies and sauté for a minute. Grind to a coarse paste along with coconut, tamarind pulp and sufficient water.
6. Heat remaining oil in a *kadai*. Add mustard seeds and curry leaves and let the mustard seeds crackle.
7. Add asafoetida and the ground *masala*. Stir well and cook for two minutes.
8. Add boiled *chana* and stir well. Add steamed jackfruit pieces, salt and jaggery. Stir, add half a cup of water and cook for five minutes on low heat stirring occasionally.
9. Remove from heat and serve hot.

Apply oil to a knife and to your hands before peeling a raw jackfruit. Further, cut into slices and then cubes using the same oiled knife. You can also use yam instead of jackfruit - the taste will be slightly different but good all the same.

Potatoes in Spicy Mangalorean Gravy

(Batata Humman)

Ingredients

4 medium sized	Potatoes
1 cup	Coconut (scraped)
4-5	Red chillies whole (*bedgi*) (roasted)
1 tbsp	Tamarind pulp
A large pinch	Asafoetida
2 medium sized	Tomatoes (1 inch sized cubes)
2 tsps	Coconut oil

Method

1. Scrub potatoes well under running water so that all the mud on the skin is washed away.
2. Boil potatoes and when cool cut into one inch sized cubes without peeling.
3. Grind together scraped coconut, roasted red chillies and tamarind pulp to a smooth paste. Add asafoetida and blend it well.
4. Mix potato cubes, tomato cubes, ground paste, half a cup of water, salt to taste and heat the mixture till it just comes to a boil on high heat. Lower heat and simmer for two to three minutes.
5. Drizzle raw coconut oil. Cover immediately and take off the heat. Let it stand for five minutes.
6. Serve hot with steamed rice or *chapatis*.

A mild gravy dish, it goes well with both rice and *chapatis*. A favourite item of *puja* menus in Saraswat Brahmin homes.

Bhindi Coconut Masala

(Bhenda Hooli)

Ingredients

500 gms	Ladyfingers (*bhindi*)(cut into ¾ inch pieces)
2 tbsps	Oil
7-8 cloves	Garlic (crushed)
For paste	
2 tsps	Oil
2-3	Red chillies whole (*bedgi*)
1 tsp	Mustard seeds
½ tsp	Fenugreek seeds (*methi dana*)
1 tsp	Coriander seeds
½ cup	Coconut (scraped)
1 tbsp	Tamarind pulp
Salt to taste	

Method

1. Heat two tablespoons of oil in a *kadai*. Add crushed garlic and sauté till golden. Add ladyfinger pieces, stir well and cook uncovered for three to four minutes.
2. Heat two teaspoons of oil in a small pan. Add whole red chillies, mustard seeds, fenugreek seeds, coriander seeds and sauté till lightly coloured. Grind this with scraped coconut into a coarse paste. Add tamarind pulp and grind again.
3. Add the ground *masala* to the ladyfingers, stir well and cook for two minutes.
4. Add two cups of water and salt to taste. Stir and cook till gravy becomes thick.
5. Serve hot.

A hot and sour Saraswat Brahmin preparation, this dish can also be made with brinjals.

Sweet and Sour Tomatoes

(Tomato Panchamrit)

Ingredients

250 gms	Ripe tomatoes (½ inch pieces)
2 tsps	Oil
¼ tsp	Mustard seeds
2-3	Green chillies (slit)
A pinch	Asafoetida
¼ tsp	Turmeric powder
Salt to taste	
2 tsps	Jaggery (grated)
¼ cup	Peanuts (roasted & crushed)
A few sprigs	Fresh coriander leaves (chopped)

Method

1. Heat oil in a *kadai* and add mustard seeds. When they crackle, add green chillies. Sauté for half a minute and add asafoetida and turmeric powder.
2. Add tomato pieces, salt and jaggery and stir to mix well. Cover, reduce heat and cook till the tomatoes become soft.
3. Add crushed roasted peanuts and mix well.
4. Garnish with chopped coriander leaves and serve hot.

An easy-to-make tangy dish, it goes especially well with *chapatis*.

Sweet and Sour Tomatoes

Bhindi Coconut Masala

Banana Flower Bhaji

Tender Coconut & Cashewnut Sukke

Tender Coconut and Cashewnut Sukke

(Shahala ani Kajuche Sukke)

Ingredients

1 cup	Tender coconut flesh (2 inch x ¼ inch slices)
25-30	Cashewnuts (soaked for 1 hour)
1 tbsp	Oil
½ tsp	Cumin seeds
3-4 cloves	Garlic (crushed)
1 large sized	Onion (chopped)
5-6	Curry leaves
2 medium sized	Tomatoes (chopped)
½ tsp	Turmeric powder
1 tsp	Red chilli powder
Sea salt to taste	
3 tbsps	Tomato puree
2 tbsps	Coconut (scraped)
½ cup	Coconut milk (thick)
A few sprigs	Fresh coriander leaves (chopped)

Method

1. Heat oil in a pan and add cumin seeds, crushed garlic and chopped onion. Sauté.
2. Add curry leaves to the slightly browned onion and stir. Add chopped tomatoes, turmeric powder, red chilli powder and cook for a while.
3. Add the soaked cashewnuts and a little water. Cook for a while, then add sea salt, tomato puree and mix.
4. Add coconut slices and scraped coconut and stir.
5. Add coconut milk and cook till almost dry.
6. Add chopped coriander leaves and mix well.
7. Serve hot.

The coconut used here is the tender flesh (*malai*) of the green coconut, which can be removed once the water is consumed.

Banana Flower Bhaji

(Kelphulachi Bhaji)

Ingredients

1	Banana flower
½ cup	Green gram split (*dhuli moong dal*)
3 tbsps	Oil
1 tsp	Cumin seeds
5-6	Curry leaves
A pinch	Asafoetida
2-3	Green chillies (finely chopped)
1½ tsp	Red chilli powder
¼ tsp	Turmeric powder
Salt to taste	
1 tsp	Jaggery (grated)
¼ cup	Coconut (scraped)
A few sprigs	Fresh coriander leaves (chopped)

Method

1. Remove outer part of banana flower, separate the inner white stalks/flowers and use these flowers for this *bhaji.*
2. Wash the thin white flowers (*kelphool*), drain and chop. Keep soaked in water overnight.
3. Soak *dhuli moong dal* in one cup of water for at least thirty minutes. Drain.
4. Heat oil in a pan and add cumin seeds. As they begin to change colour, add curry leaves, asafoetida and green chilllies. Stir well.
5. Add drained *moong dal* and sauté for a minute.
6. Add *kelphool*, mix well and add red chilli powder, turmeric powder, salt and jaggery.
7. Cover and cook till done and add scraped coconut. Mix well.
8. Serve hot garnished with chopped coriander leaves.

Besides the banana fruits, the flowers of the banana tree are also used in cooking. The tiny flowers are enclosed in reddish-purple leaves shaped like a large ear of corn. Do not use the flower if it has a green upper tip. It should be red or yellow.

Goan Mixed Vegetables

(Khadkhade)

Ingredients

½ cup	Pigeon pea split (*toor dal*)
100 gms	Red pumpkin (thick strips)
1½ medium sized	Carrots (thick strips)
15	French beans (thick strips)
1 medium sized	White radish (thick strips)
3 tbsps	Oil
½ tsp	Cumin seeds
½ tsp	Mustard seeds
½ tsp	Turmeric powder
1½ tsps	Red chilli powder
½ tsp	*Garam masala* powder
½ cup	Coconut (scraped)
Salt to taste	
For serving	
A few sprigs	Fresh coriander leaves (chopped)

Method

1. Soak *toor dal* in one and a half cups of water for half an hour. Boil it in one cup of water till half done. Drain excess liquid.
2. Heat oil in a pan, add cumin seeds and mustard seeds. When they crackle, add the boiled *toor dal* and the vegetables. Mix well.
3. Add turmeric powder, red chilli powder, *garam masala* powder, scraped coconut and salt. Stir well.
4. Add a little water, mix well and cook till vegetables are done.
5. Serve hot garnished with chopped coriander leaves.

Chef's Tip: The dish name is pronounced *khud* (where 'u' is pronounced as in 'mud') *khuday*. The combination of vegetables with *toor dal* makes this a highly nutritious and tasty preparation. It is a popular item of a typical Goan meal.

Piquant Tender Cashewnuts

(Bibbya Upkari)

Ingredients

400 gms	Tender cashewnuts (*bibbe*)
1 tbsp	Oil
½ tsp	Mustard seeds
10	Curry leaves
2-3	Red chillies whole (broken)
Salt to taste	
1 tsp	Jaggery (grated)
½ cup	Coconut (scraped)

Method

1. Soak the cashewnuts in three cups of hot water for fifteen minutes. Peel them.
2. Heat oil in a pan and add mustard seeds. When they crackle add curry leaves and broken red chillies.
3. Add the peeled cashewnuts, salt and jaggery. Stir, add half a cup of water, cover and cook till the nuts are tender and dry.
4. Garnish with scraped coconut and serve hot.

This dish is prepared with the fresh unprocessed cashewnuts and is really delicious as it brings out the raw flavour of the nut. However you can make it with regular cashewnuts too. Soak the cashewnuts overnight and then proceed with the cooking as given above. The taste will be differently delicious.

Green Peas with Coconut

(Matar Naralachi Ussal)

Ingredients

1¼ cups	Green peas (shelled)
1 cup	Coconut (scraped)
2 tbsps	Oil
½ tsp	Mustard seeds
5-6	Curry leaves
4	Green chillies (finely chopped)
1 inch piece	Ginger (finely chopped)
¼ tsp	Turmeric powder
1 tsp	Cumin powder
Salt to taste	
½ tbsp	Lemon juice
¼ small bunch	Fresh coriander leaves (finely chopped)

Method

1. Grind half a cup of scraped coconut with half a cup of water. Extract coconut milk.
2. Heat oil in a pan. Add mustard seeds and let them crackle. Add curry leaves.
3. Add green chillies and ginger. Cook for a few seconds.
4. Add green peas and remaining scraped coconut. Mix well and cook on low heat.
5. Add turmeric powder, cumin powder, salt, lemon juice and a quarter cup of water. Mix well.
6. Cover and cook till green peas are done and water is absorbed. Stir in coconut milk.
7. Serve hot, garnished with chopped coriander leaves.

Ussal is a typical dish of the Maharashtra region. In the Konkan it is prepared with coconut. The popular snack *missal* is made with *ussal* of sprouted *moong* or *matki* to which mixture or *chewda,* chopped onions, coriander leaves and lemon juice are added. It is eaten with *pav* (a kind of bread).

Colocassia Bhaji

(Aaluchi Patal Bhaji)

Ingredients

8	Colocassia leaves (*arbi ke patte*)(shredded)
¼ cup	Bengal gram split (*chana dal*)(soaked)
Salt to taste	
3 tbsps	Tamarind pulp
3 tbsps	Oil
½ tsp	Mustard seeds
5-6	Curry leaves
A generous pinch	Asafoetida
¼ tsp	Fenugreek seeds (*methi dana*)
4 cloves	Garlic (finely chopped)
4-5	Green chillies (finely chopped)
¼ tsp	Turmeric powder
3 tbsps	Gram flour (*besan*)
¼ cup	Raw peanuts
1 tbsp	Jaggery (grated)
½ cup	Coconut (scraped)

Method

1. Boil *arbi* leaves with salt, one and a half tablespoons of tamarind pulp and *chana dal* in four cups of water till done.
2. Heat oil in a pan. Add mustard seeds, curry leaves, asafoetida, fenugreek seeds, garlic and sauté for one minute. Add green chillies, turmeric powder and sauté for half a minute. Add *besan*, mix and sauté for a minute.
3. Add the boiled mixture and half a cup of water if required. Adjust salt and stir.
4. Add raw peanuts and adjust water. Cook for five minutes and add grated jaggery. Bring to a boil again and add the remaining tamarind pulp and mix.
5. Add scraped coconut and some more water if required and cook on medium heat for half an hour, stirring occasionally.
6. Serve hot.

Generally colocassia leaves are used to make *patra* (a snack) but in Maharashtra it is also made into a thin gravy which is a delicacy.

Mangalorean Potatoes

(Batata Song)

Ingredients

4 large sized	Potatoes (boiled & cubed)
2 large sized	Onions (chopped)
8-10	Red chillies whole (deseeded)
1 lemon-sized ball	Tamarind
3 tbsps	Coconut oil
Salt to taste	

Method

1. Lightly roast and grind whole red chillies with tamarind and a little water to a fine paste.
2. Heat oil in a frying pan and fry the chopped onions until light brown.
3. Add the ground paste and sauté for two to three minutes. Add the potato pieces and mix well. Add one cup of water and salt and simmer on low heat till a thick gravy is formed.
4. Serve hot with puris or *chapatis*.

Smeeta Bhatkal, our publisher's wife, makes it a bit differently. She adds one tablespoon of split black gram (*urad dal*) and one tablespoon of coriander seeds roasted in a little oil to the chillies and tamarind while grinding. The taste is obviously different but excellent all the same.

Mixed Fruits and Coconut Raita

(Fruit Sasam)

Ingredients

¾ cup	Bananas (ripe)(1 inch cubes)
½ cup	Pineapple (1 inch cubes)
½ cup	Orange segments (skinned & halved)
¼ cup	Green grapes (seedless)
½ cup	Coconut (scraped)
2	Red chillies whole (*bedgi*)(roasted)
¼ tsp	Mustard seeds
1 tsp	Tamarind pulp
1 tbsp	Jaggery (grated)
Salt to taste	

Method

1. Grind together scraped coconut, red chillies, mustard seeds, tamarind pulp and one fourth cup of water into a coarse paste. Add grated jaggery and blend once again.
2. Mix the fruit pieces with salt and ground *masala*.
3. Mix well and serve cold.

A must at Saraswat Brahmin weddings - it is made with ripe mangoes too.
The taste is simply divine.

Mixed Fruits
and
Coconut Raita

Sprouted Beans in Coconut Masala

Stuffed Chillies

Stuffed Chillies

(Bharli Mirchi)

Ingredients

8 large sized	Green chillies (*Bhavnagri*)
Salt to taste	
5 tbsps	Oil
A pinch	Asafoetida
½ tsp	Mustard seeds
1 tsp	Turmeric powder
2 cups	Coconut (scraped)
1 tsp	Red chilli powder
½ tsp	Aniseed powder
¼ tsp	Cumin powder
¼ tsp	Coriander powder
1 small sized	Raw mango (grated)
A few sprigs	Fresh coriander leaves (finely chopped)

Method

1. Slit green chillies and deseed. Apply a little salt and keep aside for thirty minutes. Wash and drain well.
2. Heat two tablespoons of oil and temper with asafoetida, mustard seeds and turmeric powder.
3. Add coconut and sauté till lightly coloured.
4. Add red chilli powder, aniseed powder, cumin powder, coriander powder and raw mango. Sauté till well mixed and dry.
5. Add salt and chopped coriander leaves. Remove from heat and set aside.
6. Stuff mixture into chillies and keep aside.
7. Heat remaining oil in a shallow pan. Place chillies, cover and cook for five minutes.
8. Remove and serve hot.

Chef's Tip: These Bhavnagri chillies are seasonal. You can make this using small capsicums - it is not authentic but they taste good.

Sprouted Beans in Coconut Masala

(Dalimbi Ussal)

Ingredients

2/3 cup	Beans (*vaal*)
¼ tsp	Turmeric powder
¼ tsp	Asafoetida
1 tsp	Mustard seeds
2 tbsps	Oil
10-12	Curry leaves
½ cup	Tamarind pulp
Salt to taste	
¾ cup	Coconut (scraped)
2-3	Green chillies (roughly chopped)
1 medium sized	Onion (chopped)
1 medium sized	Tomato (chopped)
A few sprigs	Fresh coriander leaves (chopped)
Mixture (*farsan*) as required	

Method

1. Wash *vaal* and soak overnight in two cups of water. Drain and tie the *vaal* in a muslin cloth. Leave it in a warm, dark place for a couple of days to sprout. Remove the skin before cooking.
2. Boil two cups of water and add half the turmeric powder, half the asafoetida, half the mustard seeds, two teaspoons of oil and half the curry leaves.
3. Add *vaal* and cook for fifteen to twenty minutes on medium heat till they are soft.
4. Add tamarind pulp and salt. Boil for a few more minutes.
5. Grind coconut along with the green chillies and make a fine paste.
6. Add the paste to the gravy and bring to a boil once more.
7. Heat the remaining oil in a pan and add the remaining mustard seeds, curry leaves, asafoetida and turmeric powder. When the seeds splutter, pour this tempering over the gravy and stir well.
8. Garnish with chopped onion, tomato and coriander leaves, along with a generous helping of *Farsan*.
9. Serve hot along with toasted *Pav* or sliced bread.

Vaals are oval shaped beans, flat, very light brown in colour with a white eye. After sprouting the skin should be removed as it is very bitter. The bitter taste however lingers but when cooked with other ingredients it turns into a delicacy.

Konkan Cookbook - Sanjeev Kapoor

Stuffed Brinjals

(Bharli Vangi)

Ingredients

8-10	Small brinjals (*vangi*)
1 lemon sized ball	Tamarind
¾ cup	Coconut (scraped)
¼ medium bunch	Fresh coriander leaves (chopped)
4 tbsps	Oil
2 medium sized	Onions (thinly sliced)
¼ cup	Dry coconut (grated)
2 tbsps	Sesame seeds (*til*)
¼ cup	Peanuts
½ tsp	Cumin seeds
1 tsp	Coriander seeds
2 tsps	*Goda masala*
Salt to taste	
¼ tsp	Turmeric powder
1½ tsps	Red chilli powder
½ tsp	Mustard seeds
6-8	Curry leaves

Method

1. Wash and slit brinjals into four, keeping the stems intact. Keep in water.
2. Soak tamarind in half a cup of warm water for half an hour. Remove the pulp, strain and keep aside.
3. Reserve one tablespoon each of the scraped coconut and chopped coriander leaves for garnish.
4. Heat one tablespoon of oil in a pan and add onions. Stir-fry briefly.
5. Add grated dry coconut, sesame seeds, peanuts, cumin seeds, coriander seeds and sauté on medium heat for two minutes, stirring continuously till dry coconut changes to light golden in colour.
6. Cool and grind to a coarse paste adding a little water. Combine this paste with *goda masala*, salt, turmeric powder, red chilli powder, fresh scraped coconut, chopped coriander leaves and tamarind pulp. Stuff this prepared mixture into the brinjals.
7. Heat remaining oil in a pan. Add mustard seeds and let them crackle. Add curry leaves and gently place stuffed brinjals.
8. Cook for two to three minutes. Gently turn brinjals once or twice to ensure even cooking. Add one cup of water and bring it to a boil.
9. Reduce heat and cook covered for eight to ten minutes or till brinjals are cooked and soft. Most of the stuffing will leave the brinjals and form the gravy for the dish.
10. Serve hot, garnished with reserved coriander leaves and scraped coconut.

Note: For the recipe of Goda masala see page no. 137

The small, dark purple brinjals are used for this dish. The best way to test good quality brinjals is that they should feel light for their size.

Cauliflower and Potato Sukke

(Cauliflower Ani Batata Sukke)

Ingredients

½ medium sized	Cauliflower (florets)
2 large sized	Potatoes (cut into cubes)
2 tbsps	Oil
1 tbsp	Black gram split (*dhuli urad dal*)
2 tsps	Coriander seeds
¼ tsp	Fenugreek seeds (*methi dana*)
3	Red chillies whole (*bedgi*)
½ cup	Coconut (scraped)
½ tsp	Tamarind pulp
½ tsp	Mustard seeds
1 sprig	Curry leaves
A pinch	Asafoetida
¼ tsp	Turmeric powder
1 medium sized	Onion (finely chopped)
Salt to taste	

Method

1. Heat one teaspoon of oil in a pan. Add *dhuli urad dal* and sauté for half a minute. Add coriander seeds, *methi dana* and red chillies and sauté till a nice aroma is given out taking care that the spices do not burn. Grind with scraped coconut, tamarind pulp and three tablespoons of water to a coarse paste.
2. Heat remaining oil in a *kadai.* Add mustard seeds. When they crackle, add curry leaves, asafoetida and turmeric powder. Add chopped onion and sauté till golden.
3. Add potato cubes, stir well and cover with lid and cook for three to four minutes.
4. Remove lid and add cauliflower. Stir well again. Cover and cook for seven to eight minutes on low heat till done.
5. Remove lid. Add coconut *masala*, half a cup of water and salt to taste. Stir well and cook for two to three minutes.
6. Serve hot.

This can be made with a combination of other vegetables also. It has a thick and coarse texture and goes well with *chapatis.*

Peas and Potatoes in Coconut Masala

(Vatana Ani Batata Ambat)

Ingredients

¾ cup	Green peas (shelled) (boiled)
3 medium sized	Potatoes (boiled, 1 inch cubes)
¾ cup	Coconut (scraped)
1 medium sized	Onion (finely chopped)
2 tsps	Coriander seeds
4	Red chillies whole
1 tsp	Tamarind pulp
3-4 cloves	Garlic
1½ tbsps	Coconut oil
¼ tsp	Turmeric powder
Salt to taste	
½ inch piece	Ginger (finely chopped)
1	Green chilli (finely chopped)

Method

1. Grind scraped coconut, one tablespoon of chopped onion, coriander seeds, whole red chillies and tamarind pulp with a little water. Add garlic cloves and continue grinding to a fine paste.
2. Heat oil in a deep pan, add remaining chopped onion and sauté till golden.
3. Add boiled green peas, boiled potato cubes, turmeric powder and stir well.
4. Add the coconut *masala*, two cups of water and salt to taste. Bring to a boil and then reduce heat and simmer for three to four minutes. Adjust consistency. The gravy should not be too thick or too thin.
5. Garnish with finely chopped ginger and green chilli and serve hot.

The well-liked combination of green peas and potatoes cooked in a coconut gravy in Mangalorean style tastes as good as the popular *alu-matar*.

Sweet and Sour Pumpkin

(Dudhiya Khotkhotein)

Ingredients

250 gms	Red pumpkin (1 inch cubes, with skin)
¼ cup	Coconut (scraped)
3-4	Red chillies whole (*bedgi*)(roasted)
1 tsp	Coriander seeds
6-8 cloves	Garlic
1 tsp	Tamarind pulp
6-7	*Triphal* (pitted)
Salt to taste	
1½ tsps	Jaggery (grated)
1 tbsp	Oil

Method

1. Grind together coconut, roasted red chillies, coriander seeds, three cloves of garlic and tamarind pulp. Grind the *triphal* with one-fourth cup of water. Strain and use only the water.
2. Cook the pumpkin pieces in a steamer. Transfer them into a pan.
3. Add salt and jaggery. Add the ground *masala* and *triphal* water and mix well.
4. Allow to simmer on low heat till it comes to a boil.
5. Heat oil in a pan. Crush the remaining garlic cloves and add to the hot oil and fry till reddish brown. Add this tempering to the dish, mix well and serve hot.

The spicy coconut *masala* with a predominant flavour and goodness of *triphal* makes this red pumpkin dish extra tasty. It has an unusual flavour.

Konkan Cookbook - Sanjeev Kapoor

Spicy Tindora

(Tendlya Butti)

Ingredients

250 gms	Tindli (*tindora*)(chopped)
2 tbsps	Oil
2 medium sized	Onions (chopped)
1 tbsp	Jaggery (optional)
Salt to taste	
For paste	
½ cup	Coconut (scraped)
Lemon size ball	Tamarind
4-5	Red chillies whole (roasted)
1 tbsp	Coriander seeds

Method

1. Grind together coconut, tamarind, whole red chillies and coriander seeds with a little water into a coarse paste.
2. Heat oil in a *kadai*. Add chopped onions and sauté till reddish brown.
3. Add *tindli* and sauté for two minutes. Add salt to taste and stir. Cover and cook on low heat till the *tindli* is almost done.
4. Add ground *masala* and continue to sauté on low heat till the *masala* turns brown and almost all the water is absorbed. Add jaggery (if using) and stir.
5. Remove from heat and serve hot.

This dish is another favourite from the vast repertoire of Mangalorean cuisine. The slow cooking on low heat is what gives it a special flavour.

Tangy Potato Curry

(Ambat Batata)

Ingredients

5-6 medium sized	Potatoes (boiled & peeled)
3 tbsps	Oil
½ tsp	Mustard seeds
1 tsp	Cumin seeds
6-7	Curry leaves
3	Green chillies (finely chopped)
3 medium sized	Onions (finely chopped)
½ tsp	Turmeric powder
½ cup	Yogurt (whisked)
4-5 petals	*Kokum*
¼ medium bunch	Fresh coriander leaves (finely chopped)
¼ cup	Coconut (scraped)
Salt to taste	
2 tsps	Lemon juice

Method

1. Halve each potato and further cut each half into four equal sized pieces.
2. Heat oil in a pan. Add mustard seeds and let them crackle. Add cumin seeds and stir-fry briefly. Add curry leaves, green chillies and stir. Immediately add chopped onions and sauté till golden brown in colour.
3. Add turmeric powder, potato cubes and stir-fry for one to two minutes. Stir in yogurt, *kokum* pieces, half the chopped fresh coriander leaves and half the scraped coconut, salt and lemon juice. Reduce heat and simmer for one to two minutes.
4. Garnish with the remaining chopped coriander, remaining scraped coconut and serve hot.

The lip-smacking spicy and tangy taste makes this Maharashtrian dish extra special.

Konkan Cookbook
Sanjeev Kapoor

MAIN COURSE
SEAFOOD

Prawn Balchao

(It can be had as a pickle too)

Ingredients

2¼ cups	Prawns (shelled & deveined)
Salt to taste	
2 one-inch pieces	Ginger (roughly chopped)
15-20 cloves	Garlic (roughly chopped)
1 tsp	Cumin seeds
12-15	Red chillies whole
10-12	Cloves
2 one inch sticks	Cinnamon
1 tsp	Mustard seeds
1 cup	Malt vinegar
¾ cup	Oil
2 large sized	Onions (finely chopped)
4 large sized	Tomatoes (chopped)
2 tbsps	Sugar

Method

1. Wash the prawns thoroughly, drain excess water and pat dry with a kitchen towel. Add salt and keep aside.
2. Grind ginger, garlic, cumin seeds, whole red chillies, cloves, cinnamon and mustard seeds along with vinegar into a fine paste.
3. Heat oil in a *kadai* and sauté the prawns till all the moisture dries up. Remove prawns and keep aside. In the same oil sauté onions till they turn soft and light brown. Add chopped tomatoes and cook on high heat till it forms a thick pulp and the oil surfaces.
4. Add the ground *masala* and stir-fry for two to three minutes. Add the prawns and sugar. Check seasoning and cook on low heat for five to seven minutes more or till oil leaves the *masala*.
5. Serve hot with *pav* or boiled rice.

A very popular Goan dish, Prawn Balchao lasts long and tastes better with passing time.

Surmai Bhaji

(Surmaichi Bhaji)

Ingredients

½ kg	King fish (*surmai*)(1 inch thick slices)
4 petals	*Kokum*
10-12 cloves	Garlic
1 inch piece	Ginger
5-6	Green chillies
a few sprigs	Fresh coriander leaves (chopped)
1 tsp	Red chilli powder
½ tsp	Turmeric powder
Salt to taste	
2-3 tbsps	Oil
3 medium sized	Onions (finely chopped)
¼ cup	Coconut (scraped)

Method

1. Soak *kokum* in one-fourth cup of water for half an hour. Strain the water and keep aside.
2. Combine garlic, ginger, green chillies, coriander leaves, red chilli powder, turmeric powder and salt along with a little water to make a thick paste.
3. Apply this *masala* to the fish pieces and keep aside for fifteen minutes.
4. Heat oil in a thick-bottomed pan. Add onions and fry till golden brown.
5. Add the marinated fish pieces and sauté for a minute stirring lightly.
6. Add *kokum* water and cover and cook on low heat for three to four minutes or till oil surfaces on top and most of the moisture is absorbed.
7. Garnish with scraped coconut, stir lightly and serve hot with *chapatis*.

A typical Malvani preparation, this dry dish goes very well with simple *dal* and rice.

Tangy Prawns

(Ambat Kolambi)

Ingredients

2 cups	Prawns (shelled and de-veined)
2 tbsps	Oil
5-6 cloves	Garlic (crushed)
2	Green chillies (sliced)
1 tsp	Red chilli powder
½ tsp	Turmeric powder
2 tbsps	Tamarind pulp
Salt to taste	
A few sprigs	Fresh coriander leaves (finely chopped)

Method

1. Heat oil in a *kadai*. Add garlic and green chillies and sauté on medium heat for a minute.
2. Add prawns, red chilli powder and turmeric powder and continue to sauté for two minutes.
3. Add tamarind pulp and salt along with half a cup of water and bring to a boil.
4. Reduce heat, add chopped coriander leaves and simmer for two minutes. Serve hot.

Simple but tasty - this dish is a sure winner.

Konkan Cookbook - Sanjeev Kapoor

Crab Sukhe

(Kurlya Sukhe)

Ingredients

4 medium sized (300 gms each)	Crabs
1 lemon sized ball	Tamarind
4 tbsps	Oil
3 medium sized	Onions (finely sliced)
1 inch piece	Ginger (finely sliced)
12-16 cloves	Garlic (finely sliced)
1½ cups	Coconut (scraped)
½ tsp	Mustard seeds
6-7	Curry leaves
½ tsp	Turmeric powder
1 tsp	*Malvani masala*
1 tsp	Red chilli powder
Salt to taste	
A few sprigs	Fresh coriander leaves (finely chopped)

Method

1. Clean crabs and wash thoroughly. Detach and crack the claws.
2. Soak tamarind in one cup of warm water for half an hour, remove the pulp, strain and keep aside.
3. Heat one tablespoon of oil in a pan and fry sliced onions, sliced ginger, garlic and scraped coconut till light golden brown.
4. Remove from heat and cool. Add a little water and grind into a thick paste.
5. Heat remaining oil in a pan. Add mustard seeds. When they start to crackle, add curry leaves. Immediately add *masala* paste and cook on medium heat for half a minute, stirring continuously.
6. Add turmeric powder, *Malvani masala*, red chilli powder, tamarind pulp and salt. Stir well and add one cup of water. Bring it to a boil and add crab pieces and claws.
7. Cook further on medium heat for ten to fifteen minutes, stirring occasionally or till the gravy becomes a little thick.
8. Serve hot garnished with chopped coriander leaves.

Note: For tips on how to handle crabs see page no. 136. For the recipe of Malvani Masala see page no. 138

Whatever be the appearance of the crabs, when cooked the delicate flavours intermingling with the spices linger on.

Sour & Hot Surmai

(Ambat Tikhat Surmai)

Ingredients

1 medium sized (750 gms)	King fish (*surmai*)(1 inch thick pieces)
Salt to taste	
4 petals	*Kokum*
5-6	*Triphal* (pitted)
10	Red chillies whole
2 tsps	Coriander seeds
1 cup	Coconut (scraped)
½ tsp	Turmeric powder
4 tsps	Tamarind pulp
4 tbsps	Oil
A few sprigs	Fresh coriander leaves (chopped)

Method

1. Apply salt to fish pieces and set aside for fifteen minutes. Soak *kokum* in half a cup of hot water for fifteen minutes. Strain and use the water. Grind *triphal* in a quarter cup of water and strain. Use only the water.

2. Grind together whole red chillies, coriander seeds, scraped coconut and turmeric powder to a fine paste with half a cup of water. Add tamarind pulp, *triphal* water and one tablespoon of oil. Apply this *masala* to the fish pieces and set aside for half an hour.

3. Heat the remaining oil. Add fish pieces along with the *masala* and sauté for one minute. Add half a cup of water. Reduce heat, cover the vessel with a lid and pour a little water over it. Cook for ten minutes and remove lid.

4. Add *kokum* water and bring to a boil. Add more water if necessary as the gravy should be quite thin. Adjust salt.

5. Garnish with chopped coriander leaves and serve hot with steamed rice.

As the name suggests this dish has the punch that will win over the most discerning palate.

Clams in Coconut Gravy

(Tisryanche Kalvan)

Ingredients

2 cups (400 gms)	Clams (*tisrya*)
Salt to taste	
½ tbsp	Lemon juice
½ cup	Coconut (scraped)
3 tbsps	Oil
2 medium sized	Onions (finely chopped)
1 tbsp	Ginger paste
1 tbsp	Garlic paste
¼ tsp	Turmeric powder
½ tbsp	Tamarind pulp
A few sprigs	Fresh coriander leaves (chopped)

For *masala*

1 tbsp	Oil
2 medium sized	Onions (thinly sliced)
5-6	Cloves
7-8	Peppercorns
2 one inch sticks	Cinnamon
½ tsp	Caraway seeds (*shahi jeera*)
1 tsp	Coriander seeds
5-6	Red chillies whole
¼ cup	Dry coconut (grated)

Method

1. Clean and wash clams. Apply salt and lemon juice. Keep aside for fifteen minutes.
2. For *masala*, sauté sliced onions in one tablespoon of oil till golden brown. Dry roast cloves, peppercorns, cinnamon, caraway seeds, coriander seeds, whole red chillies and dry coconut separately. Mix with browned onions and grind to a very fine paste, adding one-fourth cup of water.
3. Add half a cup of warm water to the scraped coconut. Grind and squeeze out thick milk. Keep it aside.
4. Heat three tablespoons of oil in a vessel. Add chopped onions, sauté till light golden brown.
5. Add ginger paste and garlic paste. Sauté for a few seconds. Add ground *masala*, sauté on low heat for two to three minutes. Add one and a half cups of water and bring it to a boil.
6. Add clams, turmeric powder, coconut milk and tamarind pulp. Cook, covered, for five to seven minutes.
7. Garnish with chopped coriander leaves and serve the *tisryanche kalvan* preferably with steamed rice.

Note: For tips on how to handle clams see page no. 136.

This dish can be made with mussels too. Both clams and mussels are types of shellfish. But whereas clams are rounder and smaller in size with a light brown shell that has light black streaks, mussels are longer and bigger with black shells. The meat of the clams is whitish whereas the meat of the mussels is blackish. The taste too is different.

Crab Masala

(Kurlya Masala)

Ingredients

6 (meduim sized)	Crabs
2 tbsps	Oil
2	Bay leaves
3-4	Peppercorns
2	Cloves
2	Green cardamoms
4-5 medium sized	Onions (finely chopped)
½ tsp	Turmeric powder
½ - 1 tsp	Red chilli powder
For green *masala*	
1 small sized bunch	Fresh coriander leaves
4-5	Green chillies
2 tbsps	Ginger (grated)
2 tbsps	Garlic (grated)
2	Cloves
6	Peppercorns
½ inch stick	Cinnamon
For coconut *masala*	
2 tbsps	Oil
1 tbsp	Coriander seeds
2	Peppercorns
2	Cloves
½ inch stick	Cinnamon
1 inch stick	Cinnamon
1 medium sized	Onions (sliced)
1½ cups	Coconut (scraped)

Method

1. Grind all the ingredients of the green *masala* into a fine paste using about one-two tablespoons of water.
2. For the coconut *masala,* heat two tablespoons of oil in a pan. Add coriander seeds, peppercorns, cloves and cinnamon and sauté them for two minutes. Add onions and continue to sauté till the onions turn pink.
3. Add coconut and continue to sauté on very low heat till the coconut turns brown taking care that it does not get burnt. Cool this mixture and grind to a very fine paste using half a cup of water.
4. Heat two tablespoons of oil in a *kadai*. Add bay leaves, peppercorns, cloves and green cardamoms and sauté for two minutes. Add the green *masala* and sauté till a nice aroma is given out. Add finely chopped onions and sauté till the oil leaves the *masala*.
5. Add turmeric powder and red chilli powder and sauté for a couple of minutes more.
6. Add the prepared crabs and mix well. Add one cup of water and salt to taste. Bring it to a boil. Lower the heat and cook till the crabs are done.
7. Add the coconut *masala* and half a cup of water and mix well. Adjust seasoning. Once the gravy comes to a boil take it off the heat and keep it covered for about five minutes.
8. Serve hot with steamed rice or *chapatis*.

Note: For tips on how to prepare crabs see page no. 136.

A speciality of our friend Mrs. Mangaonkar, this is the best Crab *Masala* I have ever had!

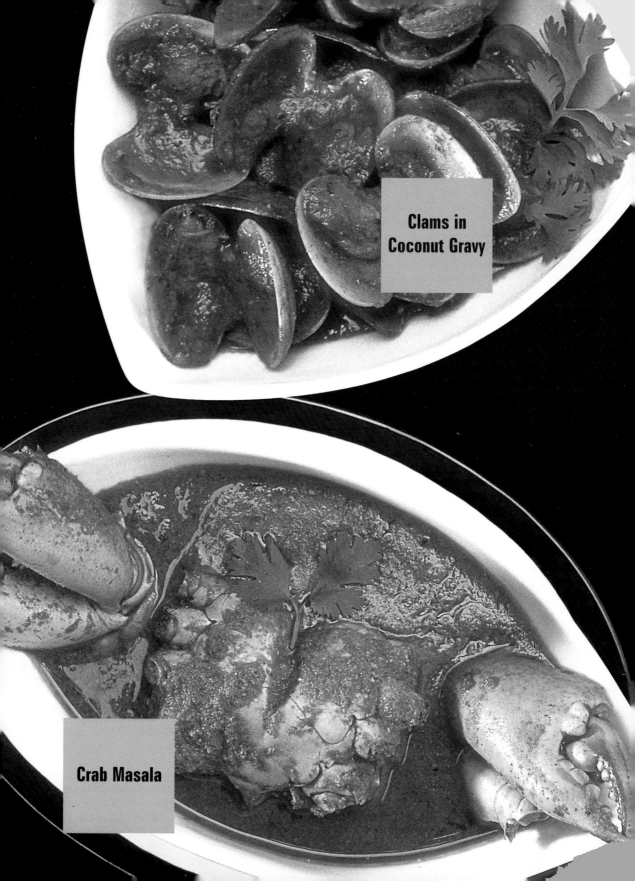

Clams in Coconut Gravy

Crab Masala

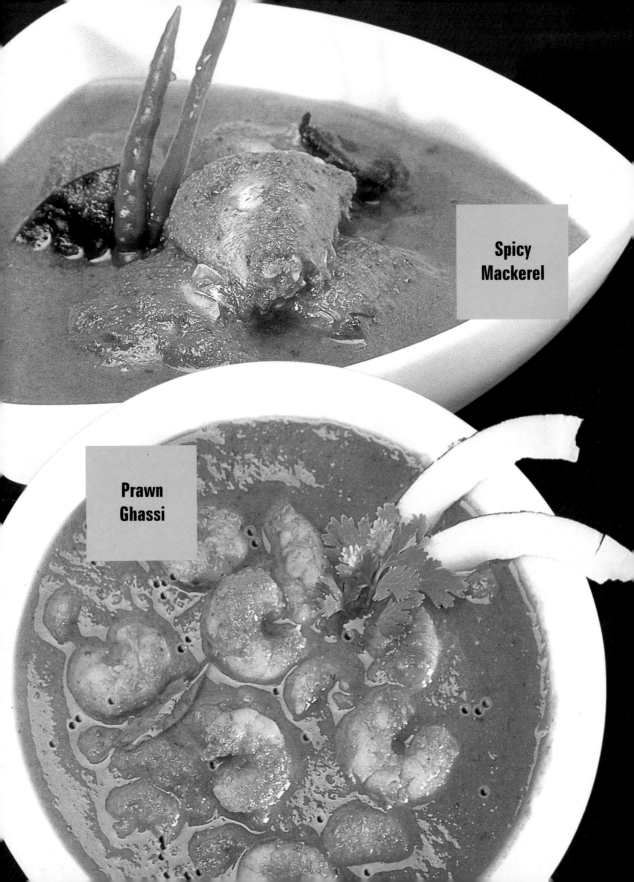

Spicy
Mackerel

Prawn
Ghassi

Mackerels in Coconut Gravy

(Bangdyache Humman)

Ingredients

4 medium sized (200 gms each)	Mackerels (*bangda*)(cut into 4 pieces each)
1 ⅓ cups	Coconut (scraped)
4	Red chillies whole
½ tsp	Turmeric powder
1 tbsp	Tamarind pulp
10-12	*Triphal* (pitted)
Salt to taste	
2	Green chillies (slit)
3 petals	*Kokum*

Method

1. Apply salt to the fish pieces and keep aside for about fifteen minutes.
2. Grind coconut, red chillies, turmeric powder and tamarind pulp to a fine paste with sufficient water.
3. Grind the *triphal* with half a cup of water and strain. Use only the water.
4. Mix together ground paste, *triphal* water, salt, slit green chillies and two cups of water and cook till the mixture comes to a boil. Lower heat and simmer for two to three minutes.
5. Add the mackerel pieces and cook for about three to four minutes. Add *kokum* petals and take off the heat. Cover and keep for about fifteen minutes before serving with boiled rice.

This mildly spiced Mangalorean dish is a good complement to a spicy starter.

Prawn Ghassi

(Probably the most popular Mangalorean seafood gravy)

Ingredients

18-20 medium sized	Prawns (shelled & de-veined)
Salt to taste	
1 cup	Coconut (scraped)
2 medium sized	Onions (finely chopped)
4	Red chillies whole (roasted)
2 tsps	Coriander seeds
1 tsp	Cumin seeds
8 - 10	Peppercorns
¼ tsp	Fenugreek seeds (methi dana)
½ tsp	Turmeric powder
5 cloves	Garlic
1½ tbsps	Tamarind pulp
3 tbsps	Oil

Method

1. Wash prawns thoroughly under running water. Drain and pat them dry. Sprinkle salt and keep aside for one hour preferably in the refrigerator.
2. Grind scraped coconut, half the chopped onions, whole red chillies, coriander seeds, cumin seeds, peppercorns, fenugreek seeds, turmeric powder, garlic and tamarind pulp to a smooth paste using sufficient water and keep aside.
3. Heat oil in a *kadai* and fry the remaining chopped onions till light brown.
4. Add ground *masala* paste and sauté for two to three minutes. Add two cups of water and mix well. When the mixture comes to a boil add prawns and adjust seasoning.
5. Simmer for five minutes or till cooked. Serve hot.

This is a favourite at many seafood restaurants. You might add a tempering of mustard seeds and curry leaves. It adds flavour though it is not traditionally used.

Malvani Masala Pomfret

(Malvani Masala Paplet)

Ingredients

2 medium sized (400 gms each)	Pomfret (1 inch thick slices)
2 tsps	*Malvani masala*
1 large sized	Onion (sliced)
8-10	Red chillies whole
½ cup	Coconut (scraped)
1 tbsp	Coriander seeds
3 tbsps	Oil
¼ tsp	Turmeric powder
1½ tbsps	Tamarind pulp
Salt to taste	
6-8 cloves	Garlic (crushed)
½ tsp	Red chilli powder

Method

1. Lightly fry sliced onion, red chillies, scraped coconut and coriander seeds with one tablespoon of oil for two to three minutes. Remove from heat. When cool, grind to a paste along with turmeric powder, tamarind pulp, salt and half a cup of water.
2. Apply the ground *masala* to the fish pieces and leave to marinate for fifteen minutes.
3. Heat remaining oil in a thick-bottomed pan, add garlic and sauté on medium heat for a minute.
4. Add red chilli powder and *Malvani masala* along with two to three tablespoons of water and fry for a minute.
5. Add the fish pieces and one-fourth cup of warm water and cover and cook on medium heat for ten minutes or till oil surfaces on top, stirring lightly.
6. Serve hot with *rotis*.

Note: For the recipe of Malvani Masala see page no. 138.

Fiery yet flavoursome, this is the way Mrs. Nirmala Sawant makes it! A must try.

Goan Fish Curry

(A traditional favourite)

Ingredients

2 medium sized (400 gms each)	Pomfret or any flat fish
2 tbsps	Oil
1 small sized	Onion (chopped)
2	Green chillies (slit & halved)
Salt to taste	
1 tbsp	Malt vinegar
For paste	
2 tsps	Cumin seeds
2 tbsps	Coriander seeds
6	Red chillies whole
½ cup	Coconut (scraped)
2 inch piece	Ginger (chopped)
15 cloves	Garlic (chopped)
2 tbsps	Tamarind pulp

Method

1. Clean, wash and cut each fish into five to six pieces.
2. Dry roast cumin seeds, coriander seeds and whole red chillies.
3. Make a fine paste of the roasted spices along with scraped coconut, ginger, garlic and tamarind with a little water.
4. Apply half of the ground paste to fish.
5. Heat oil in a pan. Add chopped onion and sauté till golden brown. Add green chillies and cook on medium heat for three minutes. Stir constantly.
6. Add the remaining ground paste and stir well. Sauté for five minutes till a nice aroma is given out. Add one and a half cups of water. Bring to a boil and then add the marinated fish pieces and salt. Cook on low heat for about five minutes or till fish is just done.
7. Stir in vinegar and serve hot with steamed rice.

Served with steamed rice, you can make a full meal of this. For best results serve it with Goan rice which is smaller, rounder and brownish in colour.

Sour & Hot Pomfret

(Fish Ambotik)

Ingredients

2 medium sized (400 gms each)	Pomfrets (½ inch thick slices)
Salt to taste	
1 tsp	Turmeric powder
1 tbsp	Coriander seeds
1 tsp	Cumin seeds
1 cup	Coconut (scraped)
8-10	Red chillies whole
1 inch piece	Ginger (roughly chopped)
8-10 cloves	Garlic (roughly chopped)
5	Cloves
2 one inch sticks	Cinnamon
1½ tbsps	Vinegar
3 tbsps	Oil
2 medium sized	Onions (finely chopped)
4-5	Green chillies (slit)
1½ tbsps	Tamarind pulp

Method

1. Marinate the fish with salt and turmeric powder.
2. Dry roast coriander seeds and cumin seeds. Grind coconut, whole red chillies, cumin seeds, coriander seeds, ginger, garlic, cloves, cinnamon and vinegar to a very fine paste with a little water.
3. Heat oil in a pan. Add chopped onions and sauté till golden brown. Add ground *masala* and cook on high heat for two minutes stirring continuously.
4. Add three cups of water and bring the gravy to a boil. Add slit green chillies and stir.
5. Add the marinated fish pieces and simmer for five minutes. Add tamarind pulp and adjust salt. Stir gently and cook on low heat for five minutes.
6. Serve hot with steamed rice.

Ambo means sour and *tik* means pungent - a Goan favourite, you can also make this lip-smacking dish with mackerels or *surmai*.

Pomfret Recheiado

(Crisp Portuguese style fish)

Ingredients

2 large sized (600 gms each)	Pomfrets
Salt to taste	
1 tbsp	Lemon juice
¼ tsp	Turmeric powder
Oil to shallow fry	
2	Lemons (wedges)
1 medium sized	Onion (rings)
For the *masala* paste	
8	Red chillies whole
½ tsp	Cumin seeds
5 - 6	Peppercorns
4 - 5	Cloves
½ inch stick	Cinnamon
8 cloves	Garlic
1 inch piece	Ginger
2 tbsps	Vinegar
½ tsp	Sugar
Salt to taste	

Method

1. Wash, clean and pat dry fish. Make diagonal slits on either sides of the fish using a sharp knife. Rub salt, lemon juice, turmeric powder inside and outside of the fish. Keep aside for half an hour, preferably in the refrigerator.
2. Combine all the ingredients of the *masala* and grind to a smooth paste, using little water if required.
3. Apply the paste on both the sides of the fish and keep aside for fifteen minutes, preferably in the refrigerator.
4. Heat oil in a pan and shallow-fry the fish till crisp on both sides.
5. Serve hot with lemon wedges, onion rings and *chutney* of your choice.

It is fiery but oh so delicious! For best results serve it with a mild gravy and rice.

Mackerel Gravy

(Bangda Udadmethi)

Ingredients

4 medium sized (200 gms each)	Mackerels (*bangda*) (cut into 4 pieces each)
4 tbsps	Oil
4 tsps	Rice
4 tsps	Black gram split (*dhuli urad dal*)
3 medium sized	Onions (sliced)
1¼ cups	Coconut (scraped)
⅓ tsp	Fenugreek seeds (*methi dana*)
3	Peppercorns
½ tsp	Turmeric powder
6	Red chillies whole
4 tsps	Tamarind pulp
Salt to taste	

Method

1. Apply salt to the fish pieces and wash after fifteen minutes.
2. Heat one tablespoon of oil in a pan. Stir-fry rice till it becomes dark brown. Drain and keep aside.
3. To the same oil add *dhuli urad dal* and stir-fry till browned. Drain and mix it with roasted rice. Cool and grind to a coarse powder.
4. In a separate pan sauté one sliced onion in one and a half tablespoons of oil till golden brown. Add freshly scraped coconut and stir-fry till brown. Drain and keep aside.
5. Heat one teaspoon of oil, add fenugreek seeds and peppercorns. Stir-fry till fenugreek crackles. Cool and grind to a fine powder.
6. Grind stir-fried coconut and onions along with turmeric powder, red chillies and tamarind to a rough paste and keep aside.
7. Heat the remaining oil in a pan and add remaining sliced onions. Sauté for a while till the onions are soft. Add ground coconut paste and two cups of water.
8. Bring it to a boil. Add salt, fenugreek-peppercorn powder and mix well.
9. Add fish pieces to the gravy and let it boil for a few minutes.
10. Add rice and *urad dal* powder and mix well and cook for one to two minutes on high heat till the gravy thickens.
11. Serve hot with steamed rice.

A flavoursome gravy from Goa, while the roasted rice powder adds body to the gravy, the roasted *urad dal* and *methi* add a wonderful flavour.

Caldinho

(Medium spiced pomfret with
coconut and tamarind)

Ingredients

2 medium sized (400 gms each)	Pomfret (1 inch thick slices)
2 cups	Coconut (scraped)
1 tbsp	Coriander seeds (roasted)
½ tsp	Cumin seeds (roasted)
½ inch piece	Ginger (roughly chopped)
4-5 cloves	Garlic (roughly chopped)
3 tbsps	Oil
2 medium sized	Onions (sliced)
2	Green chillies (slit)
1 large sized	Tomato (sliced)
Salt to taste	
1 tbsp	Tamarind pulp

Method

1. In a blender, combine scraped coconut, coriander seeds, cumin seeds, ginger and garlic along with two cups of warm water and grind to a fine paste. Put this mixture through a fine sieve or a muslin cloth and extract all the spiced coconut milk.
2. Heat oil in a thick-bottomed pan. Add fish slices and lightly sauté on both the sides. Drain and keep aside.
3. In the same oil add onions and sauté on medium heat till light golden.
4. Add green chillies and sliced tomato and sauté for a minute.
5. Add the spiced coconut milk and simmer for two to three minutes.
6. Add sautéed fish and salt. Cover and cook on low heat for five minutes or till done.
7. Add tamarind pulp, stir gently and simmer for a minute. Serve hot with boiled rice.

This dish is versatile as you may cook prawns in place of fish, or a combination of prawns, oysters and mussels using the same *masala*. You can also substitute seafood with slices of white pumpkin for vegetarians.

Malvani Prawn Masala

(Malvani Kolambi Sukhe)

Ingredients

1 cup	Prawns (*kolambi*)(shelled & de-veined)
Salt to taste	
½ tbsp	Lemon juice
3 tbsps	Oil
1 tsp	Cumin seeds
4-5	Curry leaves
1 medium sized	Onion (finely chopped)
2 medium sized	Tomatoes (finely chopped)
½ cup	Coconut milk
¼ tsp	Turmeric powder
½ tsp	Dry *Malvani masala* (optional)
A few sprigs	Fresh coriander leaves (chopped)
For paste	
2 medium sized	Onions (sliced)
¼ cup	Dry coconut (grated)
3-4	Dry *Sankeshwari* chillies
2	Black cardamoms
2	Green cardamoms
3-4	Cloves
1 inch stick	Cinnamon
1	Star anise
1	Stone flower (*dagad phool*)
2 tsps	Coriander seeds
½ tsp	Cumin seeds

Method

1. Marinate prawns with salt and lemon juice.
2. Roast sliced onions in two teaspoons of oil on a *tawa* till light golden brown.
3. Roast grated dry coconut on hot *tawa* until light golden brown. Keep aside.
4. Dry roast *Sankeshwari* chillies, black cardamoms, green cardamoms, cloves, cinnamon, star anise, *dagad phool*, coriander seeds and cumin seeds one by one.
5. Grind all ingredients into a fine paste with a little water.
6. Heat remaining oil in a pan. Add cumin seeds, cook until slightly brown, add curry leaves and chopped onion. Continue cooking until onion turns golden brown.
7. Add chopped tomatoes and cook till the tomatoes are completely mashed.
8. Add ground paste and sauté for three to four minutes. Add prawns and mix well.
9. Cook on low heat for five to six minutes. Add coconut milk, turmeric powder and dry *Malvani masala* (if using). Adjust salt and mix well.
10. Cook further for two to three minutes and serve hot, garnished with chopped coriander leaves.

Chillies come in different sizes and degrees of spiciness. The smaller they are the spicier. The bigger chillies give the colour whereas the smaller ones give the pungent punch.

**Konkan
Cookbook**
Sanjeev Kapoor

MAIN COURSE CHICKEN AND MUTTON

Chicken in Malvani Green Masala

(Malvani Chicken Hirwa Masala)

Ingredients

1 medium sized (800 gms)	Chicken (skinned, cut into 16 pieces)
Salt to taste	
1 tbsp	Ginger-garlic paste
¾ cup	Coconut (scraped)
4 tbsps	Oil
½ inch stick	Cinnamon
2	Black cardamoms
2	Green cardamoms
1	Bay leaf
2-3	Cloves
½ tsp	Cumin seeds
3 medium sized	Onions (finely chopped)
½ tsp	*Garam masala* powder
A few sprigs	Fresh coriander leaves (chopped)
For *hirwa masala*	
½ small bunch	Fresh coriander leaves (chopped)
½ cup	Coconut (scraped)
½ inch piece	Ginger (roughly chopped)
4	Green chillies (roughly chopped)

Method

1. Apply salt and ginger-garlic paste to the chicken pieces and leave aside for half an hour.
2. Grind scraped coconut with a quarter cup of warm water and extract thick milk.
3. Grind together the ingredients of *hirwa masala* to a fine paste.
4. Heat oil in a pan. Add cinnamon, black cardamoms, green cardamoms, bay leaf, cloves and cumin seeds. When they crackle, add chopped onions and cook until soft and translucent.
5. Add *hirwa masala* paste. Sauté on low heat for two to three minutes.
6. Add chicken pieces and further cook for two to three minutes.
7. Add half a cup of water, adjust salt and cook until chicken is done.
8. Finally add coconut milk and *garam masala* powder. Mix well.
9. Garnish with chopped coriander leaves and serve hot.

An aromatic, tasty dish - highly recommended for those who like it mild.

Chicken Ghassi

(Kori Ghassi)

Ingredients

800 gms	Chicken (1 inch pieces)
1½ tbsps	Lemon juice
1½ tbsps	Ginger-garlic paste
½ tsp	Turmeric powder
Salt to taste	
1½ cups	Coconut (scraped)
1½ tbsps	Coriander seeds
15	Peppercorns
½ tsp	Fenugreek seeds (*methi dana*)
1½ tsps	Cumin seeds
10	Red chillies whole (*bedgi*) (deseeded)
3 tbsps	Oil
3 medium sized	Onions (finely chopped)
½ tsp	Mustard seeds
10	Curry leaves
8	Garlic (finely chopped)
1½ tbsps	Tamarind pulp
¾ cup	Coconut milk

Method

1. Marinate chicken with lemon juice, ginger-garlic paste, turmeric powder and salt for an hour.
2. Dry roast scraped coconut to a light brown. Lightly sauté coriander seeds, peppercorns, fenugreek seeds, cumin seeds and whole red chillies in two teaspoons of oil. Grind these along with roasted scraped coconut and half the chopped onions to a fine paste using a little water if required.
3. Heat remaining oil in pan. Add mustard seeds and curry leaves. When the seeds crackle, add chopped garlic and onion and sauté for five minutes on low heat.
4. Add ground *masala* and sauté for five minutes till a nice aroma is given out.
5. Add marinated chicken. Stir well and add one cup of water and adjust salt. Stir, cover and cook for ten minutes.
6. Add tamarind pulp and stir well. Add coconut milk and remove from heat just when it comes to a boil.
7. Serve hot.

Note: For the recipe of coconut milk see page no.138

The roasted spices give this dish an inimitable Mangalorean touch.

Chicken Cafreal

(Goan Roast Chicken in Green Masala)

Ingredients

1 (1 kg)	Chicken (cut into 8 pieces)
3 tbsps + to deep fry	Oil
2 medium sized	Onions (finely sliced)
1 tbsp	Coriander seeds
1 tsp	Cumin seeds
6	Cloves
8	Green cardamoms
8	Peppercorns
1 inch stick	Cinnamon
1 inch piece	Ginger (roughly chopped)
4-5 cloves	Garlic (roughly chopped)
6	Green chillies (roughly chopped)
Salt to taste	
3 tbsps	Vinegar

Method

1. Make deep incisions on the chicken pieces using a sharp knife.
2. Heat sufficient oil in a *kadai* and deep fry onions till crisp and golden brown. Drain on an absorbent paper and reserve for garnish.
3. Dry roast coriander seeds, cumin seeds, cloves, green cardamoms, peppercorns and cinnamon. Grind ginger, garlic, green chillies and roasted spices to a fine paste using a little water.
4. Add salt to the paste and apply this paste to the chicken and refrigerate for two to three hours.
5. Heat three tablespoons of oil in a pan, add the marinated chicken and cook covered on medium heat stirring occasionally. Add a little warm water if required to avoid scorching. Cook for eight to ten minutes.
6. When almost done add vinegar and cook for two to three minutes.
7. Serve hot garnished with fried onions.

If you like you can add a little fresh coriander leaves to the paste. I know of a restaurant in Goa which does it and it tastes delicious.

Spicy Coondapur Chicken

(Coondapur Koli Thalna)

Ingredients

1 (1 kg)	Chicken (2 inch pieces)
2 tbsps	*Ghee*
2 cups	Coconut milk
2 medium sized	Onions (finely chopped)
Salt to taste	
2 tbsps	Lemon juice
For paste	
2 tsps	Oil
7-8	Red chillies whole
1 tbsp	Coriander seeds
1 tsp	Cumin seeds
7-8	Peppercorns
½ tsp	Fenugreek seeds (*methi dana*)
½ cup	Coconut (scraped)
8-10 cloves	Garlic
1 tsp	Turmeric powder

Method

1. Lightly roast whole red chillies, coriander seeds, cumin seeds, peppercorns and fenugreek seeds in two teaspoons of oil. Grind to a fine paste along with coconut, garlic, turmeric powder and half a cup of water.
2. Heat one tablespoon of *ghee* in a thick bottomed pan. Add half of the chopped onions and ground paste. Sauté for two minutes then add chicken, coconut milk, salt and lemon juice. Cover and cook for ten to fifteen minutes or till the gravy thickens.
3. Heat remaining *ghee* in a pan. Add remaining chopped onions and sauté till light golden brown. Add the cooked chicken and half a cup of water and cook for five more minutes.
4. Serve hot.

Note :For the recipe of coconut milk see page no. 138.

Simply delicious with rice *wadas.*

Mangalorean Chicken

(Kori Ajadina)

Ingredients

1 (1 kg)	Chicken (1 inch pieces)
2 tbsps	Lemon juice
Salt to taste	
3 tbsps	Oil
1 inch stick	Cinnamon
4-5	Cloves
3-4	Peppercorns
1	Bay leaf
10	Curry leaves
1 inch piece	Ginger (finely chopped)
5-6	Garlic (finely chopped)
2 medium sized	Onions (finely chopped)
1 cup	Coconut (scraped)
¼ small bunch	Fresh coriander leaves (finely chopped)
3 medium sized	Tomatoes (finely chopped)
For *masala* powder	
1 inch stick	Cinnamon
3	Cloves
1-2	Green cardamoms
4-5	Peppercorns
1 tsp	Poppy seeds (*khuskhus*)
1 tsp	Cumin seeds
1 tbsp	Coriander seeds
½ tsp	Fenugreek seeds (*methi dana*)
6	Kashmiri red chillies
5	Madras red chillies
½ tsp	Turmeric powder

Method

1. Marinade chicken with lemon juice and salt for half an hour preferably in a refrigerator.
2. Dry roast all the ingredients of the *masala* powder very lightly. Cool and grind to a powder.
3. Heat oil in a *kadai*. Add cinnamon, cloves, peppercorns and bay leaf. Sauté for half a minute and add curry leaves.
4. Add ginger and garlic. Sauté for a couple of minutes. Add onions, stir well and sauté till golden brown.
5. Add ground *masala* powder, stir well and add scraped coconut and half of the chopped coriander leaves. Stir well and cook for five minutes till a nice aroma is given out. Add tomatoes, stir well and cook for five minutes till tomatoes are soft.
6. Add marinated chicken. Stir, add half a cup of water, cover and cook for ten minutes or till the chicken is cooked.
7. Remove from heat and garnish with the remaining coriander leaves. Serve hot.

This pungent dish incorporates the flavours of a wide variety of spices - the result is amazing.

Goan Chilli Chicken

(Some like it hot!)

Ingredients

8	Chicken thighs
1 small sized	Onion (roughly chopped)
2 one-inch pieces	Ginger (roughly chopped)
4 cloves	Garlic (roughly chopped)
6	Green chillies (chopped)
Salt to taste	
4 tsps	Lemon juice
1 tsp	Cumin seeds
2 tbsps	Coriander seeds
2	Red chillies whole
4	Green cardamoms
4	Cloves
1 inch stick	Cinnamon
4 tbsps	*Ghee*
4 tbsps	Tomato puree
¼ tsp	Sugar
A few sprigs	Fresh coriander leaves (chopped)
1 tbsp	Vinegar

Method

1. Clean chicken thighs and remove the skin. Wash and drain thoroughly.
2. Make a paste of onion, ginger, garlic and half of the chopped green chillies.
3. Add salt and lemon juice to this paste and marinate chicken pieces in it for two hours, preferably in a refrigerator.
4. Dry roast cumin seeds, coriander seeds, whole red chillies, green cardamoms, cloves, cinnamon and grind to a powder.
5. Heat two tablespoons of *ghee* in a pan. Add the marinated chicken pieces and cook on high heat.
6. Once the chicken is cooked a bit, add the dry *masala* powder and mix well.
7. Add the remaining *ghee* and tomato puree and let it cook.
8. Add sugar and adjust salt and cook till the chicken is done.
9. Add the remaining chopped green chillies and chopped coriander leaves.
10. Remove from heat. Add vinegar, stir and serve immediately.

This Goan version of chilli chicken is irresistible.

Goan Chilli Chicken

Chicken Xacuti

Chicken Xacuti

(A traditional favourite)

Ingredients

1 (800 gms)	Chicken (skinned & cut into 12 pieces)
⅓ cup	Oil
1 cup	Coconut (scraped)
2 one inch sticks	Cinnamon
6	Cloves
4	Red chillies whole
½ tsp	Turmeric powder
2 tbsps	Poppy seeds (*khuskhus*)
1 tsp	Carom seeds (*ajwain*)
1 tsp	Cumin seeds
10	Peppercorns
1 tsp	Fennel seeds (*saunf*)
4	Star anise (*phoolchakri/badiyan*)
1½ tbsps	Coriander seeds
4-6 cloves	Garlic (peeled)
2 medium sized	Onions (finely chopped)
Salt to taste	
1 tbsp	Tamarind pulp
¼ tsp	Nutmeg (grated)

Method

1. Heat one tablespoon of oil in a pan and slightly brown the scraped coconut and keep aside.
2. Dry roast cinnamon, cloves, whole red chillies, turmeric powder, poppy seeds, carom seeds, cumin seeds, peppercorns, fennel seeds, star anise and coriander seeds till a nice aroma is given out. Grind to a paste together with garlic and roasted coconut with three-fourth cup of water.
3. Heat the remaining oil in a thick-bottomed pan and sauté onions till brown.
4. Add the *masala* paste and cook till oil separates. Add the chicken pieces and sauté for two to three minutes. Add two cups of water and salt. Bring to a boil.
5. Simmer for five minutes. Add tamarind pulp, grated nutmeg and mix well. Serve hot with *pav* (a kind of bread) or steamed rice.

The word xacuti is pronounced 'shakuti'. An all-time favourite of Goan food lovers, it is a sell out in most Goan restaurants. I first learnt this dish in 1984 when we hosted a team of Goan chefs in our hotel for a food festival.

Chicken in Cashewnut Gravy

(Dhurandari Chicken)

Ingredients

1 (800 gms)	Boneless chicken (1 inch pieces)
16	Cashewnuts
½ cup	Pineapple juice
4 tbsps	*Ghee*
1 tbsp	Ginger paste
1 tbsp	Garlic paste
¾ tsp	Pepper powder
6-8	Green chillies (finely chopped)
¼ tsp	Cinnamon powder
Salt to taste	
½ small bunch	Fresh coriander leaves (chopped)

Method

1. Boil cashewnuts in one cup of water. Drain and grind into a paste with pineapple juice.
2. Heat *ghee* in a pan. Add ginger paste, garlic paste, pepper powder, green chillies and chicken.
3. Sauté for five minutes. Add one and a half cups of water, stir, cover and cook.
4. When chicken is almost done, add pineapple and cashewnut paste, cinnamon powder, salt and mix well. Continue cooking.
5. When chicken is done, serve hot garnished with chopped coriander leaves.

Malvani cuisine is associated with spicy, pungent preparations. This dish, however, is mild yet with a rich gravy.

Malvani Mutton

(Spicy Mutton Curry)

Ingredients

800 gms	Mutton (1 inch cubes on the bone)
5 tbsps	Oil
4 medium sized	Onions (finely sliced)
1½ tbsps	Ginger paste
1½ tbsps	Garlic paste
Salt to taste	
¾ tsp	Turmeric powder
A few sprigs	Fresh coriander leaves (chopped)

For *masala*

12	Red chillies whole
3 tsps	Coriander seeds
6-8	Cloves
7-8	Peppercorns
¾ tsp	Cumin seeds
¾ tsp	Caraway seeds (*shahi jeera*)
6	Green cardamoms
4	Black cardamoms
¾ cup	Dry coconut (grated)
1½ tsps	Poppy seeds (*khuskhus*)

Method

1. Dry roast red chillies, coriander seeds, cloves, peppercorns, cumin seeds, caraway seeds, green cardamoms, black cardamoms, grated dry coconut and poppy seeds separately on a hot *tawa*.
2. Mix all the roasted ingredients and grind to a fine paste with a little water.
3. Heat oil in a thick-bottomed vessel. Add onions and sauté till light golden brown.
4. Add the ginger and garlic pastes. Sauté for a few seconds.
5. Add the mutton pieces. Sauté for a few minutes and add four cups of water and salt to taste. Let it cook, covered, on low heat.
6. Once the mutton is cooked, add the ground *masala*, turmeric powder and mix well. If the gravy is too thick, add another half a cup of water and simmer for two to three minutes.
7. Check the seasoning. Serve hot, garnished with coriander leaves.

I don't eat too much mutton nowadays but it is difficult to resist this fiery dish from the Malvan coast.

Mutton Sukha

(Mutton with thick gravy)

Ingredients

800 gms	Mutton (1½ inch cubes on the bone)
1½ tbsps	Ginger-garlic paste
1½ tbsps	Lemon juice
Salt to taste	
4 tbsps	Oil
2 medium sized	Onions (finely chopped)
A few sprigs	Fresh coriander leaves (finely chopped)

For *masala*

½ medium bunch	Fresh coriander leaves
¼ medium bunch	Fresh mint leaves
3 large sized	Onions (roughly chopped)
7	Green chillies
1½ inch piece	Ginger (roughly chopped)
10 cloves	Garlic
3	Red chilles whole
3 tsps	Sesame seeds
1½ tbsps	Coriander seeds (roasted)
6	Cloves
1½ inch stick	Cinnamon
3	Green cardamoms

Method

1. Clean mutton. Marinate with ginger-garlic paste, lemon juice and salt for an hour. Cook in a pressure cooker with two cups of water for ten to fifteen minutes. Strain the mutton pieces.
2. Grind all the ingredients of the *masala* into a fine paste.
3. Heat oil in a *kadai*. Add chopped onions and sauté for few minutes till light golden brown.
4. Add ground *masala* and sauté for five to eight minutes. Add mutton and adjust salt. Stir well and cook for five more minutes till mutton is fully done.
5. Garnish with coriander leaves and serve hot.

A favourite of the Malvan region, Mutton Sukha can be served along with a mild gravy or with *chapatis*.

Mutton Stew

(Mutton in thin coconut curry)

Ingredients

800 gms	Mutton (1 inch pieces on the bone)
3 medium sized	Potatoes (1 inch cubes)
2 cups	Coconut (scraped)
1½ tbsps	Coriander seeds
1½ tsps	Cumin seeds
15	Peppercorns
1½ inch stick	Cinnamon
6	Cloves
1½ tbsps	Lemon juice
5	Green chillies (chopped)
7-8	Garlic (chopped)
4 tbsps	*Ghee*
4 medium sized	Onions (finely chopped)
3 medium sized	Tomatoes (finely chopped)
Salt to taste	
½ small bunch	Fresh coriander leaves (chopped)

Method

1. Pressure cook mutton with three cups of water till four whistles. Drain mutton pieces and keep the stock aside.
2. Dry roast three tablespoons of scraped coconut, coriander seeds, cumin seeds, peppercorns, cinnamon and cloves till a nice aroma is given out.
3. Grind these to a fine paste with lemon juice, green chillies, garlic and a little water.
4. Grind the remaining scraped coconut with one cup of water. Strain through a muslin cloth to get one cup of thick coconut milk.
5. Heat *ghee* in a thick-bottomed pan. Add onions and sauté till light brown.
6. Add the mutton pieces and potato cubes to the onions and continue to sauté for five minutes. Add the reserved stock and simmer till the potatoes are done.
7. Add the ground *masala* and mix well. Add tomatoes and salt to taste. Simmer for five minutes.
8. Add the coconut milk and take off the heat just when it comes to a boil.
9. Serve hot garnished with chopped coriander leaves.

A thin gravy which goes well with Neer Dosa - a Mangalorean favourite.

Konkan Cookbook
Sanjeev Kapoor

DALS

Sprouted Beans in Coconut Gravy

(Kirlayle Mooga Ambat)

Ingredients

¼ cup	Whole green gram (*sabut moong*)
1 tsp	Oil
¼ tsp	Fenugreek seeds (*methi dana*)
4	Red chillies whole (*bedgi*)
½ tsp	Turmeric powder
1½ cups	Coconut (scraped)
1 tbsp	Tamarind pulp
Salt to taste	
For tempering	
1 tbsp	Oil
1 small sized	Onion (finely chopped)

Method

1. Soak moong in half a cup of water for three to four hours. Drain and tie it up in a muslin cloth. Leave it in a warm, dark place for a day to sprout.
2. Boil *moong* sprouts in one and a half cups of water till it is cooked but still firm and crunchy. Set aside.
3. Heat oil in a frying pan. Add fenugreek seeds and sauté till light brown. Stir in whole red chillies and turmeric powder and remove from heat.
4. Add it to freshly scraped coconut and grind with tamarind pulp to a fine paste. Add little water while grinding.
5. Combine the ground paste, boiled sprouts, salt and half a cup of water and bring to a boil. Keep aside. Add more water if the gravy is too thick.
6. For tempering, heat oil in a small pan. Add mustard seeds. When they crackle add curry leaves. Add chopped onion and sauté till the onion turns golden brown.
7. Pour the seasoning over the curry and cover immediately to trap the flavours.
8. Serve hot with rice.

Note: You may use one-fourth teaspoon of mustard seeds and a few curry leaves instead of the onion for tempering.

A typical Saraswat Brahmin preparation - an excellent complement to Mangalorean Potatoes (Batata Song).

Kokum Saar

(Amsul Saar)

Ingredients

8-10 petals	*Amsul / kokum*
1 inch piece	Ginger (chopped)
2	Green chillies (slit)
1 cup	Coconut milk
Salt to taste	
½ tsp	Sugar
For tempering	
1 tbsp	*Ghee*
¼ tsp	Cumin seeds
3 cloves	Garlic (chopped)

Method

1. Boil *amsul* petals with three and a half cups of water, chopped ginger and slit green chillies for fifteen minutes.
2. Remove from heat and strain it.
3. Add coconut milk, salt and sugar. Stir lightly and bring to a boil.
4. Heat *ghee* in a pan. Add cumin seeds. When they start changing colour, add chopped garlic and sauté till light golden brown. Pour the tempering into the cooked *amsul saar*. Mix well.
5. Serve piping hot.

Note: For the recipe of coconut milk see page no. 138.

A mild digestive, it has thin gravy which can be served with steamed rice. I however like to drink it like a soup.

Sprouted
Beans in
Coconut Gravy

Kokum
Saar

Spicy
Coconut Gravy

Black Peas in
Spicy Gravy

Black Peas in Spicy Gravy

(Kale Vatanyachi Amti)

Ingredients

1½ cups	Black peas (*kale vatane*)(soak overnight)
3 medium sized	Onions (1 sliced & 2 finely chopped)
2 tbsps	Oil
2 tbsps	Dry coconut (grated)
4-5 cloves	Garlic
¼ cup	Coconut (scraped)
A pinch	Asafoetida
½ tsp	Turmeric powder
1 tbsp	Red chilli powder
1 tsp	Cumin powder
1 tsp	Coriander powder
Salt to taste	
4 petals	*Kokum*
1 tsp	Jaggery (optional)(grated)
1 tsp	*Garam masala* powder
A few sprigs	Fresh coriander leaves (chopped)

Method

1. Heat one tablespoon of oil and sauté sliced onion till pink. Add grated dry coconut and sauté till pink. Add garlic cloves and sauté.
2. Cool and grind to a fine paste with a little water. Grind three-fourths of the fresh scraped coconut separately.
3. Heat remaining oil in a pan. Add asafoetida and finely chopped onions and sauté on high heat till onions are golden.
4. Add turmeric powder, red chilli powder, cumin powder, coriander powder and soaked black peas and stir.
5. Add three cups of hot water, salt and bring it to a boil. Cover and cook over low heat till black peas are done.
6. Add *kokum*, coconut-onion paste and fresh coconut paste. Mix well and let it simmer for two to three minutes.
7. Add a little jaggery (optional). Add *garam masala* powder and mix well.
8. Add chopped coriander leaves.
9. Garnish with the remaining scraped coconut and serve hot with rice *wadas.*

Spicy and tasty - a hit with vegetarians! Care should be taken that the peas are completely cooked as otherwise they may cause flatulence.

Spicy Coconut Gravy

(Jeermeera Kadhi)

Ingredients

1 cup	Coconut (scraped)
2 tsps	Oil
1 tsp	Cumin seeds
7-8	Peppercorns
2	Red chillies whole (*bedgi*)
2 tbsps	Tamarind pulp
Salt to taste	
For tempering	
1 tsp	Oil
8 cloves	Garlic (finely chopped)

Method

1. Heat oil in a pan. Add cumin seeds and sauté till it starts to change colour. Add peppercorns and whole red chillies. Sauté for a few seconds and remove from heat.
2. Grind it along with scraped coconut to a fine paste. Add tamarind pulp and grind again.
3. Add two cups of water and salt to taste. Bring to a boil.
4. For tempering, heat oil in a small pan. Add chopped garlic and sauté till the garlic becomes golden brown.
5. Add to the *kadhi* and cover immediately to trap the flavour. Serve hot with boiled rice.

A light gravy with a distinctive cumin seed flavour, this dish is easy on the stomach.

Kulith Saar

(Kulta Saar)

Ingredients

1½ cups	Horse gram (*kulith*)
10 cloves	Garlic
2-3	Red chillies whole (*bedgi*) (roasted)
1 small lemon-sized ball	Tamarind
1 tsp	Coriander seeds
½ tsp	Jaggery (grated)
Salt to taste	
1 tbsp	Coconut oil

Method

1. Wash and soak horse gram overnight in three cups of water. Pressure cook in the water in which the gram had been soaked. Strain the water and use it to prepare *saar*. Cooked gram may be used to make *ussal.*
2. Peel four garlic cloves and grind with roasted red chillies, tamarind, coriander seeds and two teaspoons of cooked horse gram and a little water to make a fine paste.
3. Add jaggery, salt and the ground *masala* to the strained *kulith* water. Add one cup or a little more water to get a thin consistency. Bring it to a boil.
4. Heat oil, crush the remaining six cloves of garlic with peel and sauté till light brown. Add it to the *saar* and cover immediately to trap the flavours. Stir and serve hot.

Note: This type of preparation can be made using any pulse. If you do not like the flavour of coconut oil you can use refined groundnut oil.

Kulith is a red coloured pulse different from the red *lobia*. It is very small and flat and comes in two varieties - one that is dark red in colour and one that is lighter in colour. For this dish use the darker variety. Slow cooking on low heat gives the best results.

Maharashtrian Toor Dal

(Toorichi Gode Varan)

Ingredients

½ cup	Pigeon pea split (*toor dal*)
Salt to taste	
1 tbsp	Jaggery
1	Lemon (sliced)
Tempering	
1 tbsp	*Ghee*
A pinch	Asafoetida
¼ tsp	Turmeric powder

Method

1. Soak *toor dal* in one and a half cups of water for half an hour. Drain and cook it with one and a half cups of water till fully cooked. Combine it with jaggery and whisk well to get a smooth consistency.
2. Cook over low heat, add half a cup of water and salt and bring to a boil. Add asafoetida and turmeric powder. Simmer for two to three minutes and take it off the heat. The consistency should be thick.
3. As an option, a tempering of *ghee*, asafoetida and turmeric powder could be given instead of adding it earlier.
4. Serve hot with boiled rice with a dollop of pure *ghee* and a squeeze of lemon.

Varan and rice is an integral part of a traditional Maharashtrian meal.

Spicy Dal

(Triphalanchi Amti)

Ingredients

½ cup	Pigeon pea split (*toor dal*)
8	*Triphal* (pitted)
1 large sized	Onion (chopped)
1 tsp	Red chilli powder
¼ tsp	Turmeric powder
1 tsp	Tamarind pulp
1 tbsp	Coconut (scraped)
2	Kashmiri red chillies
5	Peppercorns
Salt to taste	
½ tsp	Sugar
1 tbsp	Coconut oil
A few sprigs	Fresh coriander leaves (chopped)

Method

1. Grind the *triphal* in half a cup of water and strain. Use only the water.
2. Soak the *toor dal* in one and a half cups of water for half an hour. Drain and cook *toor dal* in a pressure cooker along with one-third of the chopped onion, red chilli powder, turmeric powder, two and a half cups of water till pressure builds up. Reduce heat and cook for a further ten minutes.
3. Grind half of the remaining onion, tamarind pulp, scraped coconut, Kashmiri red chillies, peppercorns along with salt and sugar to a fine paste. Use a little water if necessary.
4. Add the ground paste to the cooked *dal* and mix well.
5. Heat coconut oil in a *kadai*. Add the remaining onion and sauté till almost brown.
6. Add the cooked *dal* mixture and *triphal* water. Add more water if necessary to get the required consistency and bring to a boil.
7. Serve garnished with chopped coriander leaves.

Maharashtrian cuisine boasts of a variety of *amtis* using different *dals* and pulses. It is an excellent accompaniment to steamed rice.

Toor Dal Ross

(Dal Tadka Khatta Meetha)

Ingredients

½ cup	Pigeon pea split (*toor dal*)
1	Drumsticks (2 inch pieces)
5	*Triphal* (pitted)
¼ cup	Coconut (scraped)
¾ tsp	Red chilli powder
A pinch	Turmeric powder
½ tbsp	Tamarind pulp
Salt to taste	
½ tsp	Jaggery (grated)

Method

1. Soak *toor dal* in one and a half cups of water for half an hour. Drain and cook *toor dal* in one and a half cups of water till completely cooked. Whisk to get a smooth texture.
2. Cook drumstick pieces in one cup of water till done. Drain.
3. Grind *triphal* in one-fourth cup of water. Strain and keep the water.
4. Grind coconut, red chilli powder, turmeric powder and tamarind pulp to a smooth paste adding a little water.
5. Add the ground *masala*, drumstick pieces, *triphal* water to the whisked *dal* and mix well. Add one cup of water, salt to taste and jaggery and mix well. Bring the mixture to a boil. Reduce heat and simmer for three to four minutes.
6. Serve hot with boiled rice.

A typical Goan *dal* with the flavours of *triphal*.

Raw Mango Gravy

(Kairichi Amti)

Ingredients

1 medium sized	Raw mango (peeled & cut into 1 inch cubes)
½ cup	Coconut (scraped)
5	Kashmiri red chillies
1 tbsp	Coriander seeds
4	Peppercorns
1 tbsp	Coconut oil
1 tsp	Mustard seeds
A pinch	Asafoetida
¼ tsp	Turmeric powder
Salt to taste	
1 tbsp	Jaggery (grated)
1 cup	Coconut milk
¼ medium bunch	Fresh coriander leaves (chopped)

Method

1. Grind scraped coconut, Kashmiri red chillies, coriander seeds and peppercorns to a fine paste with half a cup of water.
2. Heat coconut oil in a pan. Add mustard seeds. When they crackle add asafoetida, turmeric powder, raw mango cubes and sauté.
3. Add salt, jaggery and one and a half cups of water and let it boil.
4. Add the ground paste to the raw mango mixture and cook till the mango is almost done. Mash lightly with a spoon.
5. Once the mango is cooked add the coconut milk and give just one boil. Take off the heat as coconut milk tends to split if heated for too long.
6. Serve garnished with chopped coriander leaves along with steamed rice.

A tangy gravy with a sweet tinge - a must during the mango season.

Spicy Peanut Gravy

(Shengdanyachi Amti)

Ingredients

1 cup	Raw peanuts
4-5 petals	*Kokum*
4	Green chillies (finely chopped)
½ tbsp	Jaggery (grated)
2 tbsps	Coconut (scraped)
Salt to taste	
2 tbsps	Fresh coriander leaves (chopped)

For tempering

2 tbsps	*Ghee*
½ tsp	Cumin seeds
4	Cloves
3 cloves	Garlic (chopped)
10	Curry leaves

Method

1. Dry roast peanuts on a hot *tawa* evenly. Cool, de-skin peanuts and grind into a dry and fine powder.
2. Soak *kokum* in half a cup of water for fifteen minutes. Crush slightly and strain the pulp.
3. Combine peanut powder, green chillies, *kokum* pulp, jaggery, half the scraped coconut, salt and four cups of water.
4. Boil the above mixture for ten minutes, if necessary add more water. (It must be of medium thick consistency).
5. Heat *ghee* in a pan. Add cumin seeds and cloves. When they begin to change colour, add chopped garlic, curry leaves and sauté till light golden brown.
6. Add this tempering to the *amti* (peanut mixture).
7. Garnish with chopped coriander leaves and remaining fresh coconut.
8. Serve hot with hot *rotis* (*polis*).

A Maharashtrian favourite - the peanuts make this dish rich in proteins. It is good specially for growing kids.

Konkan Cookbook
Sanjeev Kapoor

ACCOMPANIMENTS

Mixed Flour Dosa

(Ghavan)

Ingredients

1¾ cups	Whole wheat flour (*atta*)
¾ cup	Rice flour
Salt to taste	
½ cup	*Ghee*

Method

1. Combine wheat flour, rice flour and salt. Sieve.
2. Add required quantity of water to make a batter of thick pouring consistency.
3. Cover and leave it aside for about thirty to forty-five minutes.
4. Heat a *tawa*, apply a tablespoon of *ghee* and then pour about one-fourth ladle of batter. Spread the batter thinly into a three-inch diameter *dosa*.
5. Cook until light golden brown in colour, flip and cook till the other side is also golden brown.
6. Repeat with the remaining batter.
7. Serve hot with a *chutney* of your choice.

Quick and easy to make, it goes well with any gravy dish. Served with a *chutney* it can be had as a tea time snack too.

Cucumber Bread

(Dhondus)

Ingredients

2½ cups	Cucumber (grated)
1 cup	Rice
½ cup	Peanuts
Salt a pinch	
1 cup	Jaggery (grated)
1 tsp	Green cardamom powder
Ghee as required	

Method

1. Wash rice and drain. Dry the rice by spreading it on a towel. Dry roast the rice and grind coarsely to resemble semolina (*rava*). Lightly roast and grind the peanuts coarsely.
2. Squeeze out excess juice from the grated cucumber. The grated cucumber should now be two cups. Reserve the drained juice.
3. Combine the rice *rava*, grated cucumber and the drained juice with a pinch of salt and cook. Add a little water if the mixture is too dry. Cook till it begins to leave the sides of the pan. Add grated jaggery and mix.
4. Once the mixture becomes thick, add the coarsely ground peanuts and green cardamom powder. Mix well.
5. Pour onto a greased *thali* and let it set.
6. When quite cool, bake in an oven or roast on a nonstick *tawa* till both sides are golden brown. Cut into pieces and serve with pure *ghee*.

Note: The volume of jaggery and rice should be equal to the volume of the drained cucumber.

A Malvani preparation - light with a distinctive taste of peanuts.

Kolambi Bhaat

(Prawn Pulao)

Ingredients

1 cup	Prawns (*kolambi*)(shelled and deveined)
1½ cups	*Basmati* rice
1 tsp	Lemon juice
Salt to taste	
½ small bunch	Fresh coriander leaves (chopped)
½ cup	Coconut (scraped)
3	Green chillies (roughly chopped)
1 inch piece	Ginger (roughly chopped)
6-7 cloves	Garlic (roughly chopped)
12-15	Fresh mint leaves
3 tbsps	Oil
1 inch stick	Cinnamon
4	Black cardamoms
2	Star anise
4	Cloves
1 tsp	Cumin seeds
2 medium sized	Onions (finely chopped)
½ cup	Coconut milk

Method

1. Soak rice in three cups of water for thirty minutes. Drain and keep aside.
2. Wash prawns and marinate with lemon juice and salt.
3. Reserve one tablespoon each of coriander leaves and scraped coconut for garnish.
4. Grind green chillies, ginger, garlic, remaining coriander leaves, mint leaves and coconut to a fine paste.
5. Heat oil in a thick-bottomed *handi* and add cinnamon, black cardamoms, star anise, cloves and cumin seeds. Sauté for one minute.
6. Add onions, sauté for three to four minutes or till it turns light golden brown. Add ground *masala* paste, stir-fry for half a minute and add prawns. Sauté for two to three minutes.
7. Add soaked rice, stir gently for a minute. Stir in coconut milk.
8. Add three cups of hot water. Bring it to a boil, stirring once or twice. Cook on medium heat till water has almost dried. Reduce heat, cover and cook till rice is done.
9. Remove from heat and serve garnished with the reserved chopped coriander leaves and scraped coconut.

My wife Alyona finds this *pulao* simply irresistible.

Spicy Garlic Chutney

(Lashne Chitni)

Ingredients

8 cloves	Garlic
¾ cup	Coconut (scraped)
5	Red chillies whole (*bedgi*)(roasted)
Salt to taste	
½ tsp	Cumin seeds
2 tbsps	Tamarind pulp

Method

1. Grind garlic, coconut and roasted red chillies with very little water.
2. Add salt, cumin seeds and tamarind pulp and blend to a fine mixture.
3. Cover and store refrigerated. Best consumed in a day or two.

An excellent accompaniment for *dosas, idlis* and rice *sevai.*

Goan Idlis

(Sannas)

Ingredients

2 cups	Rice
1½ cups	Coconut (scraped)
200 ml	Toddy
1 tbsp	Sugar
Salt to taste	
Oil to grease	

Method

1. Wash and soak rice overnight.
2. Grind rice and coconut separately with toddy to make a thick batter. Mix the two batters. Add sugar and salt and mix again. If necessary add more toddy to get *idli* batter consistency.
3. Cover and leave in a warm place to ferment overnight.
4. Heat sufficient water in a steamer.
5. Lightly grease the *idli* moulds. Stir the batter gently and put a ladleful of batter into each *idli* mould and steam in the steamer on medium heat till the *sannas* are fluffy and done.
6. Serve hot. You can also serve this with a *chutney* of your choice.

Light and fluffy with a distinct flavour of toddy. The sap of the toddy palm is fermented to make toddy, which is a popular drink with an acrid taste. Toddy is often further distilled to make arrack, an alcoholic brew, which is available in varying degrees of potency.

Jawari Bhakri

(Jawari Roti)

Ingredients

2 cups + ¼ cup	*Jawari* flour
Salt to taste	
½ cup	White butter (fresh)

Method

1. Mix two cups of *jawari* flour and salt.
2. Add enough water to make soft dough. Knead well.
3. Divide into eight equal sized portions. Form each portion into a round ball.
4. Heat a *tawa* to medium hot.
5. Roll out a portion of the dough into a thin round shape using a little flour for dusting.
6. Roast it on the *tawa* until the lower side is cooked.
7. Apply a little water and then flip over and roast till the *bhakri* is well done.
8. Remove and repeat the same procedure with the remaining balls.
9. Serve hot with a dollop of fresh white butter.

Best cooked on wood fire. You should knead a little flour at a time and flatten out into *chapatis* ideally with hand.

Neer Dosa

(Great with Mutton Stew)

Ingredients

2 cups	Rice
Salt to taste	
Oil to shallow fry	

Method

1. Wash and soak rice in four cups of water for twelve hours. Drain and grind to a fine paste using half a cup of water.
2. Add salt and three and a half cups of water to get a flowing consistency.
3. Heat the *dosa tawa* and pour just enough oil to grease it.
4. Stir and pour a ladle full of batter starting from the outer edge moving towards the center so that it spreads in a thin, even layer. Do not use the ladle to spread it. Cover and cook for ten to fifteen seconds.
5. Remove carefully, fold into a triangle and serve immediately.

Soft and delicious - can be served with a spicy chicken or mutton dish. Though freshly made taste the best you can make ahead of time and keep them hot in a hot case. For a variation add coconut while grinding - they will be softer and smoother.

Goan Idlis

Neer Dosa

Jawari Bhakri

Rice Wade

Brinjal Pulao

Rice Wada

(Spiced Rice Puri)

Ingredients

2 cups	Rice flour
2 tbsps	Fennel seeds (*saunf*)
1 tbsp	Fenugreek seeds (*methi dana*)
Salt to taste	
1 small sized	Onion (grated)
Oil to deep fry	

Method

1. Boil one and a quarter cups of water along with fenugreek and fennel seeds for about five minutes to extract their flavour.
2. Strain and reheat the water. Add salt. Add rice flour and cook till it forms a dough and leaves the edges of the vessel.
3. Transfer into a bowl and add grated onion and mix well.
4. Apply oil to hands and make twelve equal sized balls of the dough. Press with hands and shape like *wadas*.
5. Heat sufficient oil in a *kadai* and deep-fry the *wadas* till golden brown and done. Drain on an absorbent paper and serve hot.
6. You can also make the *wadas* on greaseproof paper. Apply a little oil on the surface of the paper and place a dough ball. Cover with another greased paper and spread by pressing with hands or a rolling pin. Peel off paper from the top, gently remove the *wada* and deep-fry.

Traditionally rice *wadas* are paired with spicy chicken curry. However you can serve them with spicy mutton or pulse dishes too.

Brinjal Pulao

(Vangi Bhaat)

Ingredients

1½ cups	Rice
5 tbsps	Oil
1½ tbsps	Tamarind pulp
8-10	Baby brinjals (*vangi*)
1 tbsp	Bengal gram split (*chana dal*)
1 tsp	Mustard seeds
6	Red chillies whole
1 sprig	Curry leaves
2 medium sized	Onions (sliced)
4	Green chillies (slit)
½ tsp	Turmeric powder
A pinch	Asafoetida
Salt to taste	
Masala powder	
1 tsp	Peppercorns
4	Red chillies whole
½ tsp	Fennel seeds (*saunf*)
1 tbsp	Poppy seeds (*khuskhus*)
2	Cloves
2	Green cardamoms

Method

1. Wash and boil rice in plenty of water till three-fourths done. Drain well, mix two tablespoons of oil and set aside to cool.
2. Cut brinjals into four keeping the stem intact. Soak *chana dal* for about ten minutes, drain and keep aside.
3. Heat two teaspoons of oil and lightly fry the *masala* powder ingredients. Cool and grind to a coarse powder.
4. Heat the remaining oil and temper with mustard seeds, red chillies, curry leaves and soaked *chana dal*. Fry till well-roasted and light brown in colour. Add onions and sauté till it turns pink. Add green chillies and stir.
5. Add brinjals and stir-fry on high heat till it is half done. Sprinkle turmeric powder, asafoetida and salt. Mix and add tamarind pulp.
6. Add the *masala* powder and cook till brinjals are almost done.
7. Mix the rice into this thoroughly and toss over high heat.
8. Reduce heat, sprinkle two tablespoons of water, cover and cook till the rice is soft and completely cooked.

Note: You can substitute tamarind with lemon juice. Add the lemon juice after the rice is fully cooked.

The first time I had it was at a friend's place in Goa. Since then we make it very often at home and it has been a great hit with most of our guests.

Tempered Rice

(Phodnicha Bhaat)

Ingredients

2 cups	Rice (boiled)
2 tbsps	Oil
½ tsp	Mustard seeds
½ tsp	Cumin seeds
6	Curry leaves
2	Green chillies (finely chopped)
¼ tsp	Turmeric powder
¼ tsp	Red chilli powder
1 medium sized	Onion (finely chopped)
¼ cup	Peanuts (roasted & crushed)
1 tbsp	Lemon juice
Salt to taste	
¼ tsp	Sugar
A few sprigs	Fresh coriander leaves (finely chopped)

Method

1. Heat oil in a *kadai*. Add mustard seeds, cumin seeds, curry leaves and chopped green chillies and stir till the seeds start to crackle.
2. Add turmeric powder, red chilli powder and sauté, taking care that the *masala* does not burn.
3. Add onion and sauté till the onions are translucent.
4. Add rice and stir-fry till the *masala* is mixed well with rice.
5. Add peanuts, sprinkle some water on the rice and cover it for a minute on low heat.
6. Add lemon juice, salt and sugar and stir.
7. Serve immediately garnished with chopped coriander leaves.

What better way to use up leftover rice? You can make it with fresh rice too, it tastes just as good.

Rice Bhakri

(Tandulachi Bhakri)

Ingredients

2 cups + ¼ cup	Rice flour
Salt to taste	
Sesame seeds (*til*) as required	

Method

1. Mix two cups of rice flour and salt and sieve. Add sufficient warm water to make soft dough.
2. Divide dough into four portions and form them into round balls.
3. Dust a *thali* or a table top with a little of the remaining rice flour. Flatten each portion of the dough with your palm into a medium thick *bhakri*.
4. Heat a *tawa* to medium hot and place *bhakri* on it.
5. As it is being cooked, apply water on the upper surface of the *bhakri* and turn it over and cook the other side similarly.
6. When almost cooked, sprinkle *til* seeds on top.
7. The *bhakri* should be soft and fluffy. Serve hot.

Excellent with spicy chicken or mutton dishes, it needs a little practice to make a perfect *bhakri*.

Spicy Puri

(Teekhat Meetachi Puri)

Ingredients

1 cup + ¼ cup	Whole-wheat flour (*atta*)
Salt to taste	
3 tbsps	Semolina (*rava*)
2 tsps	Red chilli powder
½ tsp	Turmeric powder
1 tsp	Carom seeds (*ajwain*)
2 tbsps + to deep-fry	Oil

Method

1. Mix whole-wheat flour and salt and sieve.
2. Add semolina, red chilli powder, turmeric powder, *ajwain* and two tablespoons of oil. Mix well.
3. Add water, a little at a time and knead to make a semi-hard dough. Keep covered with a moist cloth for half an hour.
4. Divide the dough into twelve to sixteen equal sized portions. Shape them into round balls and roll out each portion into thin discs of three to four inches diameter using a little flour for dusting.
5. Heat sufficient oil in a *kadai* and deep-fry the rolled out *puris* till they are nicely puffed and turn light golden brown on both sides.
6. Drain *puris* on an absorbent paper and serve immediately.

These *puris* can be served as an accompaniment for lunch or dinner and even eaten as an evening snack with some pickle.

Konkan Cookbook
Sanjeev Kapoor

SWEETS

Coconut Karanji

(Olya Naralachi Karanji)

Ingredients

For outer layer

1 cup	Refined flour (*maida*)
1½ tbsps	Semolina (*rava*)
4 tbsps + to deep fry	*Ghee*
¼ cup	Milk

For stuffing mixture

1 cup	Coconut (scraped)
15-20	Raisins (chopped)
1 cup	Jaggery (grated)
½ tsp	Green cardamom powder

Method

1. Sieve *maida* into a bowl. Add *rava* and *ghee* and mix with fingertips till mixture resembles breadcrumbs. Knead into semi-soft dough with milk and sufficient water.
2. Once the dough is ready, cover it with a damp cloth and keep it aside for half an hour.
3. For stuffing, roast scraped coconut in a thick-bottomed *kadai* till lightly browned.
4. Add chopped raisins, grated jaggery, green cardamom powder and mix well. Let it cool.
5. Knead the dough once again and divide into twelve small balls.
6. Roll out each ball into a circle, place it in a greased *karanji* mould. Place a small portion of the prepared filling in the hollow. Apply a little water on edges, close the mould and press firmly.
7. Heat sufficient *ghee* in a *kadai* and fry the *karanjis* till crisp and golden brown on medium heat.
8. Drain on an absorbent paper and allow to cool before storing in an airtight container.

A favourite sweet made specially during Ganesh Chaturthi and Diwali. You can use sugar instead of jaggery. But I like the jaggery ones more.

Kulkuls

(A Goan Christmas sweet)

Ingredients

1¼ cups	Refined flour (*maida*)
2 tbsps	Butter
1	Egg
A pinch	Salt
3½ tbsps	Powdered sugar
3 tbsps	Coconut milk
Ghee to deep fry	
For sugar-coated *kulkuls*	
1 cup	Sugar

Method

1.   Cut butter into small pieces and keep at room temperature for a while. Break egg and separate the egg yolk.
2.   Sieve flour and salt together. Add the softened butter. Mix gently.
3.   Beat egg yolk and add to the above mixture. Mix well, but gently.
4.   Add powdered sugar and coconut milk and mix till the dough is pliable and soft.
5.   Form one centimeter sized balls from the dough. Grease the ends of a fork and flatten out the dough with it to form a rectangle with ridges. Then roll up the flattened dough from one side to the other. It should resemble a tight curl.
6.   Heat sufficient *ghee* in a deep pan and fry the *kulkuls* on medium heat, turning them over till they are light golden brown in colour. Remove and drain on an absorbent paper. Store when cool.
7.   For sugar-coated *kulkuls*, boil one cup of sugar with half a cup of water till it thickens and forms a syrup of two-thread consistency.
8.   Now toss the *kulkuls* carefully in this syrup till they are evenly coated. Remove gently. Cool and store in an airtight jar.
9.   You may even dust them with powdered sugar after they are fried.

Kulkuls are a must at Christmas - you may also use edible food colours in the dough to make colourful *kulkuls*.

Coconut Karanji

Kulkul

Kela Halwa

Sweet Croquettes

Kela Halwa

(Keli Halwa)

Ingredients

2 cups	Ripe *Rajali* banana pulp
1 cup	Sugar
4 tbsps	Pure *ghee*

Method

1. Cook banana pulp and sugar together in a thick-bottomed vessel, stirring all the time till the mixture starts thickening.
2. Add two tablespoons of *ghee* and continue to cook stirring continuously.
3. As it thickens some more, add the rest of the *ghee* and continue to cook on slow heat stirring continuously.
4. To test whether it is ready, roll a little quantity into a ball. If it does not stick to the palms it is ready.
5. Pour the mixture onto a greased *thali* and spread evenly with a greased rolling pin or the back of a flat ladle.
6. Cut into square or diamond shaped pieces when still hot but do not separate them. Leave aside to cool and then separate the pieces and store.

A Mangalorean favourite - if *rajali* bananas are not available you can use the green skinned ripe bananas too. The taste and texture will be little different but nice nevertheless.

Sweet Croquettes

(Sukrunde)

Ingredients

1¼ cups	Bengal gram split (*chana dal*)
1½ cups	Jaggery (grated)
¼ tsp	Green cardamom powder
A pinch	Nutmeg powder
Oil to deep fry	
For the batter	
1½ cups	Refined flour (*maida*)
¼ tsp	Turmeric powder
A pinch	Salt
3 tbsps	*Ghee*

Method

1. Soak *chana dal* in three cups of water for an hour. Drain and boil in three cups of water till soft. Drain excess water.
2. In a thick-bottomed pan combine *chana dal*, jaggery, green cardamom powder and nutmeg powder. Mix well and cook on low heat, stirring continuously till the mixture is dry. Cool and grind.
3. Divide this mixture into equal lemon sized portions and further shape them into croquettes.
4. Mix *maida*, turmeric powder and salt. Add *ghee* and sufficient water to make a semi-thick batter. Cover and let it rest for fifteen minutes.
5. Heat sufficient oil in a *kadai*. Dip each croquette in the batter and deep fry on medium heat till light golden.
6. Drain on an absorbent paper and serve when slightly cooled.

After making *puranpolis*, if there is extra stuffing leftover, you can make this very delicious sweet. This is a must at Saraswat Brahmin weddings.

Chana Dal Kheer

(Madgane)

Ingredients

½ cup	Bengal gram split (*chana dal*)
½ cup	Cashewnuts (halved)
1 cup	Jaggery (grated)
1½ cups	Coconut milk (thin)(freshly extracted)
2 tbsps	Rice flour
1 cup	Coconut milk (thick)(freshly extracted)
½ tsp	Green cardamom powder

Method

1. Wash and soak the *chana dal* in one and a half cups of water for an hour. Drain and cook along with cashewnuts in one cup of water till soft, taking care that the *dal* is not mashed.
2. Mix jaggery in half a cup of water and stir till the jaggery dissolves. Strain to remove any impurities. Add thin coconut milk to the jaggery water and cook on low heat till it comes to a boil.
3. Mix rice flour in half a cup of water and make a smooth paste. Add this paste to the simmering jaggery mixture and cook stirring continuously to avoid any lumps.
4. Continue to cook on low heat till the rice flour is cooked. Add cooked *dal* and cashewnuts and mix well.
5. Add the thick coconut milk and green cardamom powder. Mix well and take off the heat when the mixture comes to a boil.
6. Serve with *khotte* (a kind of *idli*).

A typical Saraswat Brahmin dessert, it is supposed to be Lord Ganesh's favourite and is made in most homes during Ganesh Chaturthi.

Steamed Coconut Pancake

(Patoli)

Ingredients

1½ cups	Rice
Salt a pinch	
Oil as required	
Pure *ghee* as required	
For stuffing	
1 cup	Coconut (scraped)
6 tbsps	Jaggery (grated)
¼ tsp	Green cardamom powder
8	Turmeric leaves

Method

1. Soak rice in four cups of water for two hours. Drain and grind into a thick paste using very little water. Add salt to taste, cover and rest the batter for an hour.
2. Cook the scraped coconut and jaggery over low heat till all the moisture dries up.
3. Lightly grease the turmeric leaves on the shiny side with oil. Flatten a little of the prepared rice batter on the greased side, put the stuffing on one side of the leaf and fold the other side of the leaf over. Similarly prepare the other *patolis*.
4. Arrange the *patolis* in a colander and cook in a steamer for ten to fifteen minutes.
5. Serve hot dribbled with pure *ghee*.

Another Saraswat delicacy. If turmeric leaves are not available, you can steam them wrapped in banana leaves too.

Konkan Cookbook - Sanjeev Kapoor

Raghavdas Laadoo

(Mouth Watering Rawa Laadoos)

Ingredients

3 cups	Fine semolina (*barik rava*)
1 cup	Coconut (scraped)
¾ cup	*Ghee*
3 cups	Sugar
1 tsp	Green cardamom powder
4 tbsps	Raisins

Method

1. Heat a *kadai* and roast the scraped coconut on low heat till reddish brown. Keep aside.
2. Heat *ghee* and roast the *rava* on low heat till light brown. Take off the heat and add in the roasted coconut and mix well.
3. Add green cardamom powder and mix well. Add the raisins, keeping aside a few to garnish.
4. Cook sugar with one and half cups of water to make a one string consistency syrup.
5. Add the *rava* mixture and mix well. Cover and keep aside till the mixture cools a little.
6. Shape into *laadoos* and decorate each *laadoo* with a raisin.
7. Store when completely cooled in an airtight container. These *laadoos* do not have a long shelf life and therefore should be consumed fast, say in two to three days.

A delicious *laadoo,* I wonder where it got this unusual name from. It is a hit with all age groups.

Mango Coconut Delight

(Amba Rasayan)

Ingredients

4-5 medium sized	Ripe mangoes (cut into small cubes)
½ cup	Jaggery (grated)
3 cups	Coconut milk
¼ tsp	Green cardamom powder

Method

1. In a large bowl combine jaggery, coconut milk and stir till jaggery dissolves.
2. Add mango pieces and green cardamom powder and stir to mix well. Serve chilled.

You can also use ripe bananas or rock melons (*kharbooz*) to make *rasayan*.

Moong Dal Fudge

(Moogori)

Ingredients

1 cup	Green gram split (*dhuli moong dal*)
A few strands	Saffron
1½ cups + 2 tbsps	Milk
6-8 tbsps	*Ghee*
½ cup	*Khoya* (grated)
1 cup	Sugar
¼ tsp	Green cardamom powder
8-10	Almonds (blanched and slivered)

Method

1. Clean and soak *moong dal* in three cups of water for two to three hours. Drain and grind coarsely.
2. Soak saffron in two tablespoons of milk and keep aside.
3. Heat *ghee* in a thick-bottomed pan. Add the ground *dal* and fry on medium heat till light golden, stirring continuously.
4. Add milk and continue to cook on low heat till all the milk is absorbed and *ghee* surfaces on top.
5. Add *khoya* and cook on low heat till *dal* and *khoya* are well blended. Remove from heat and keep aside.
6. Make a one thread consistency syrup of sugar with half a cup of water, add saffron and green cardamom powder and mix well.
7. Add the fried *dal* to the hot syrup and stir quickly till it mixes well. Serve garnished with almond slivers.

A rich and tasty sweet, it is a favourite of the Malvanis.

Stuffed Sweet Chapati

(Sanjori)

Ingredients

For covering

1½ cups	Refined flour (*maida*)
A pinch	Salt
3 tbsps	Oil
Pure *ghee* as required	

For filling

1 cup	Fine semolina (*barik rava*)
4 tsps	*Ghee*
1½ cups	Sugar
¾ cup	Milk
½ tsp	Green cardamom powder

Method

1. Mix together flour and salt. Add oil and sufficient water and knead into a soft dough. Keep it covered with a damp cloth for one to two hours.
2. For the filling, heat *ghee* in a *kadai* and lightly roast *rava*. Add sugar and stir. Mix milk with three-fourth cup of water and add to the *rava* mixture. Cook, stirring continuously, till the moisture is absorbed and the mixture forms a soft ball. Take off the heat, add green cardamom powder and mix well.
3. Let it cool and divide into medium lemon sized balls. Divide the dough into the same number of portions.
4. Grease the palms of your hands, flatten one portion of dough, place a ball of *rava* mixture in the centre, and cover it up from all sides evenly with the dough.
5. Flatten slightly, and roll it out as thinly as possible, using refined flour to dust only if required.
6. Heat a *tawa* and dry roast the *sanjoris* on medium heat, till little light brown spots appear on both sides.
7. Serve hot with pure *ghee*.

A light and delectable sweet this, you can serve it at teatime too.

Til Laddoo

(Tilache Laadoo)

Ingredients

250 gms	White sesame seeds (*til*)
¼ cup	Peanuts
¼ cup	Dry coconut (grated)
½ tsp	Green cardamom powder
250 gms	Jaggery (*chikki gur*)
½ tbsp	Pure *ghee*

Method

1.   Roast white sesame seeds in a thick *kadai* till crisp taking care that they do not change colour.
2.   Roast peanuts, cool, remove skin and make a coarse powder. Lightly roast grated dry coconut. Mix sesame seeds, peanut powder, grated dry coconut and green cardamom powder.
3.   Melt jaggery in a thick-bottomed vessel (do not add water). Stir till it melts. Strain to remove impurities. Add half a tablespoon of *ghee* and mix. Cook, stirring on low heat, till a thick syrup is formed. To test if the syrup is ready, put a drop in half a cup of cold water. If the syrup forms a semi-hard ball, the syrup is ready.
4.   Add the sesame mixture and mix well. Remove from heat. Allow to cool to a temperature at which you can handle the mixture.
5.   Grease your palms and make small marble-sized *laadoos*. Cool completely and store in airtight containers.

Note: *Laadoos* should be rolled when the mixture is still warm, as the mixture starts hardening when cool. *Tilache laadoos* should be nice and hard and one can store them in a container for ten to twelve days. If *chikki gur* is not available, you can use ordinary *gur*, but then the syrup should form a soft ball when tested.

A must during Makar Sankranti.

Rice Sevai with Coconut Milk

(Rice Sevai Ani Rassu)

Ingredients

2 cups	Rice
1 cup	Coconut (scraped)
A pinch	Salt
Ghee for greasing	
3 cups	Coconut milk
1 cup	Jaggery (grated)
¼ tsp	Green cardamom powder

Method

1. Clean and soak rice in four cups of water for four to five hours. Drain and grind the soaked rice finely with one-fourth cup of water. Transfer the batter into a large vessel, cover tightly and rest the batter in a warm place for at least eight to twelve hours to ferment.
2. Grind scraped coconut to a fine paste with one-fourth cup of water.
3. Combine the fermented rice batter, ground coconut and salt along with one cup of hot water. Mix well to make a batter of dropping consistency.
4. Steam-cook portions of the above prepared batter in greased *thalis* or containers.
5. Pass a portion of the steamed cooked mixture through a *sev* press onto a damp cloth in individual roundels or oblongs and keep covered.
6. Mix together coconut milk, jaggery and green cardamom powder and stir till jaggery dissolves.
7. Serve *sevai* along with sweetened coconut milk.

These *sevais* can be sundried and stored. They can also be made with wheat. The sundried *sevais* can be made into *sevai upma* - tastes really good.

Handling Fish With Finesse

Fish by itself is not a staple diet but in combination with rice it is a much favoured dish specially in the coastal regions. Easy and quick to cook, it imbibes the spices that are added to enhance its flavour. But care should be taken while buying fish because it spoils fast and also gets contaminated and can lead to serious stomach disorders. Let's take it in a lighter vein: If the fish smells like a fish, it is not fresh anymore. Here are some handy tips for choosing, storing and cooking fresh produce of the seas!

CHOOSE THE CHOICEST

HOW TO CHOOSE FRESH SEAFOOD: Seafood falls into four categories: seawater, freshwater, preserved fish and shellfish. All but preserved fish should be eaten as fresh as possible. Actually it is possible to judge the freshness of whole fish only. Fillets, steaks and pieces are more difficult to assess.

Freshwater fish should smell fresh and clean, while seawater fish should smell of sea.
When buying whole fish check the eyes. They should be full, moist, bright and bulging.
Avoid fish with dull, dry, shrivelled or sunken eyes.
Gills should be clean, red and bright with no traces of slime.
Body should be firm, smooth and quite stiff, not limp, floppy or lumpy.
There should be mucus on scales. The presence of scales by themselves is not the criterion.
While choosing crabs, choose an active specimen that feels heavy for its size. The smell should be fresh and not strong.
While choosing clams, avoid those that are excessively covered in mud or barnacles, or that appear to be cracked or damaged. Discard any that remains open when tapped.
While choosing shrimps, pick up those that are firm with shiny gray shells. Avoid any shrimp with black spots - a sure sign of aging.

SAFE STORAGE

HOW TO STORE FRESH FISH: After purchasing fresh fish, take them home immediately, rinse them and pat dry with paper/kitchen towels. Then place in a dish, cover with a lid or aluminum foil and store in the coldest part of the refrigerator for no longer than one day. Ungutted fish such as mackerels should be gutted immediately, then rinsed, dried and stored as above. If stored ungutted, the bacteria in the guts will multiply and will cause the fish to deteriorate rapidly.

FROZEN BUT STILL FLAVOURFUL

HOW TO USE FROZEN FISH: After purchasing take frozen fish home immediately, preferably in a cool bag. Put them straight into the freezer. Generally frozen fish should be stored for no longer than three months - but always go by the 'use-by date' on the packet. To prevent the texture and structure of fish from breaking down thaw frozen fish slowly in the refrigerator overnight before cooking. Never defrost under water, as the flavour and texture of the fish will be affected, and many of its nutrients will also be lost. Fish can be thawed at room temperature, but as this can cause naturally occurring bacteria in fish to multiply, it must be used immediately once it is thawed out. Once thawed, frozen fish should never be refrozen.

DEVEINING DEVICES

HOW TO PEEL & DE-VEIN SHRIMPS AND PRAWNS: The black vein, found in a shrimp or a prawn, is its intestinal tract. This can impart a bitter taste and is not only unpleasant to eat, it can cause stomach upsets too. They should be removed before cooking. Carefully snip the shrimp or prawn along their underside with a small pair of kitchen scissor. Then gently peel way the shell, taking care to keep the shrimp or prawn intact. The tail may be left on if wished. With a small sharp knife, make a shallow incision along the back to expose the dark intestinal vein (in some shrimps this vein may not be black and is a little more difficult to find). Remove the vein with the tip of a knife then rinse the shrimp or prawn under a cold, running tap and pat dry with paper towels.

THE COOK, CRABS AND CLAMS

HOW TO PREPARE CRABS: Live hard shell crabs are usually boiled or steamed and served whole. To kill a crab humanely, chill it by submerging it in ice, or leave it in the freezer for a couple of hours until it is comatose. When the crab is no longer moving, plunge it in a pan of boiling salted water and cook for eight to ten minutes. Alternatively, the live crab can be killed and cooked simultaneously by plunging it into a pan of boiling

salted water and cooking for eight to ten minutes. Do not boil the crab for more than twelve minutes, whatever its size.

HOW TO OPEN CLAMS AND MUSSELS: Clean the clams/mussels by soaking them in several changes of water. The easiest way to open them is by steaming them. However, this method is not suitable if they are to be eaten raw like oysters. Protect your hand with a clean towel, then cup the clam in your palm, holding it firmly. Work over the bowl to catch the juices. Very carefully insert the blade of a sharp, pointed knife between the two shells. Run the knife away from you to open the clam, twisting it to force the shells apart. Cut through the hinge attaching the shells, then use a spoon to scoop out the flesh on the bottom shell and discard the shells.

THE DONE TEST

HOW TO TEST SHRIMPS FOR DONENESS: Whether they are boiled, broiled or stir-fried (with or without shells), shrimps are cooked within three to five minutes or as soon as they turn pink. However, the very large shell-on shrimp may need one to two minutes more to cook all the way through. Test by gently squeezing the shell - the shrimp will feel firm and not squidgy. Alternatively, cut one open to see the flesh is opaque all the way through.

HOW TO TEST FISH FOR DONENESS: Fish should be cooked for the shortest time possible, as overcooking will make it tough and dry. The fish is cooked when the fish is no longer translucent, but has turned opaque virtually all the way through. The flesh of a cooked fish should flake easily.

Garam Masala Powder

Ingredients

Mace	10-12 blades
Cinnamon	8-10 one-inch sticks
Cloves	25
Green cardamoms	25
Black cardamoms	10-12
Nutmeg	2
Bay leaves	8-10
Cumin seeds	8 tsps
Peppercorns	4 tsps

Method

Lightly dry roast the ingredients one by one. Cool and grind to a fine powder.
(Makes 100 gms of garam masala powder)

Goda Masala Powder

Ingredients

Coriander seeds	1 cup
Cumin seeds	2 tbsps
Stone flower (*dagad phool*)	¼ cup
Cinnamon	6 two-inch sticks
Green cardamoms	16
Cloves	25
Caraway seeds (*shahi jeera*) ¾ tsp	
Peppercorns	¾ tbsp
Bay leaves	10-12
Nagkeshar	1 tsp
Mace	2 blades
Dry coconut (*khopra*)(grated)	3 tbsps
Sesame seeds (*til*)	1 tsp
Red chillies whole	3
Asafoetida	1 tsp

Method

Roast all the ingredients one by one in a little oil. Cool and grind to a fine powder.
(Makes 100 gms of goda masala powder.)

Malvani Masala Powder

Ingredients

Red chillies whole (*bedgi*)	50
Coriander seeds	¼ cup
Cloves	12
Peppercorns	1 tsp
Fennel seeds (*saunf*)	2 tsps
Cumin seeds	½ tsp
Caraway seeds (*shahi jeera*) ¾ tsp	
Black cardamoms	2
Cinnamon	5 two-inch sticks
Stone flower (*dagad phool*)	1½ tbsps
Nagkeshar	½ tsp
Mustard seeds	½ tsp
Turmeric stick	1 inch piece
Asafoetida	½ tsp
Nutmeg	1
Star anise	½

Method

Dry roast all the ingredients one by one. Cool and grind to a fine powder.
(Makes 80 gms of malvani masala powder.)

Pathare Prabhu Masala Powder

Ingredients

Coriander seeds	4 tbsps
Cumin seeds	2¼ tsps
Mustard seeds	2¼ tsps
Whole wheat	1 tbsp
Bengal gram split (*chana dal*)	1 tbsp
Whole red chillies	8-10
Turmeric powder	½ tsp
Fenugreek seeds (*methi dana*)	¼ tsp
Asafoetida	a small pinch
Peppercorns	30

Method

Dry roast all the ingredients, except asafoetida, one by one.
Cool and grind to a fine powder.
(Makes 100 gms of pathare parabhu masala powder)

Coconut Milk

Method

Scrape coconut. Put it in a blender. For each cup of scraped coconut, use one-fourth cup of warm water and blend it properly. Pass it through a muslin cloth/strainer pressing firmly to extract all the juice (first milk). This process can be repeated to get the second, thinner milk from the same solids.

Subscribe to www.sanjeevkapoor.com NOW

Subscribe now, get fabulous discounts! Have the benefit of saving and also enjoy free books!!

Access to more than 1000 recipes besides many other sections, which will be a rare culinary treat to any food lover. In addition to online contests, etc., you will also have opportunities to win fabulous prizes.

Sanjeev Kapoor also invites all food lovers to participate in the Khana Khazana quiz and win BIG prizes every week. Watch Khana Khazana on Zee TV, answer correctly, one simple question based on that day's episode, combine it with a favourite recipe of yours and you can be the lucky winner going places!

Type	One year Subscription to www.sanjeevkapoor.com	Sanjeev Kapoor's 3 Best Selling Books Absolutely free	Total worth	You pay (offer value)	You Save	Your Choice
Yellow Chilli	Rs.1000/-	Rs.750*	Rs.1750/-	Rs.750/- (US $ 13)+	Rs.1000/-	☐
Red Chilli	Rs.1000/-	....	Rs.1000/-	Rs.500/- (US $ 10)+	Rs.500/-	☐

* Conditions Apply

*   For subscribers requesting delivery of the free books within India an additional sum of Rs.50 (Rupees Fifty only) will be levied as delivery charges.
*   For subscribers requesting delivery outside India, additional Rs.500/- delivery charges will be levied for airmail charges on the Yellow Chilli offer.
+   Foreign exchange rates are approximate.

HURRY!!! OFFER OPEN TO FIRST 1000 SUBSCRIBERS ONLY
Choose your three free books with the Yellow Chilli subscription

Khazana of Indian Recipes	Khazana of Healthy Tasty Recipes	Khana Khazana — Celebration of Indian Cooking	Low Calorie Vegetarian Cookbook	Any Time Temptations	Best of Chinese Cooking	Microwave Cooking Made Easy	Simply Indian
MRP: Rs 250	MRP: Rs 250	MRP: Rs 250	MRP: Rs 250	MRP: Rs 225	MRP: Rs 250	MRP: Rs 250	MRP: Rs 250
☐	☐	☐	☐	☐	☐	☐	☐

I'm enclosing Cheque/DD No. _____ dated _____ for

Rs._____ (in words) _____ on

(specify bank and branch) _____

favouring Popular Prakashan Pvt Ltd, Mumbai

For Credit Cards

Charge Card ☐ VISA ☐ Master Card for Rs. _____

Credit Card No. ☐☐☐☐☐☐☐☐☐☐☐☐☐☐☐☐

Card Expiry Date ☐☐ ☐☐ Card Member's Date Birth ☐☐ ☐☐ ☐☐☐☐
            MM YY   DD   MM   YYYY

Card Member's Name _____

For ☐ Yellow Chilli Subscription ☐ Red Chilli Subscription

Name: Mr./Ms _____

Address: _____

_____

City: _____ Pin: _____ State: _____

Country: _____ Phone Res.: _____

Off.: _____ E-mail: _____

Please fill in the coupon in capital letters and mail it with your Cheque/DD to :

Popular Prakashan Pvt Ltd,
35-C, Pt. Madan Mohan Malaviya Marg,
Tardeo, Mumbai - 400 034.
Phone   : 022-24941656, 24944295
Fax   : 022-24945294
E-mail : info@popularprakashan.com
Website : www.popularprakashan.com

*Delivery subject to realisation of Cheque/DD.
Please allow two weeks for processing your subscription. Please superscribe your name and address on the reverse of the Cheque/DD.
All disputes are subject to the exclusive jurisdiction of competent courts and forums in Mumbai (India) only.

This Voucher entitles the bearer redemption of Rs.50/- against purchase of Sanjeev Kapoor's books worth minimum Rs.100/-

Valid upto June 30, 2006

This Voucher entitles the bearer redemption of Rs.50/- against purchase of Sanjeev Kapoor's books worth minimum Rs.100/-

Valid upto June 30, 2006

This Voucher entitles the bearer redemption of Rs.100/- against purchase of Sanjeev Kapoor's books worth minimum Rs.300/-

Valid upto June 30, 2006

This Voucher entitles the bearer redemption of Rs.100/- against purchase of Sanjeev Kapoor's books worth minimum Rs.300/-

Valid upto June 30, 2006

For further enquiries contact:

PopulaR
prakashan

Popular Prakashan Pvt. Ltd.
35-C, Pt. Madan Mohan Malaviya Marg, Tardeo, Mumbai-400 034
Phone: 91-22-24941656 Fax: 91-22-24945294
E-Mail: info@popularprakashan.com
Website: www.popularprakashan.com, www.sanjeevkapoor.com

TERMS AND CONDITIONS FOR REDEMPTION

1. This coupon can be redeemed against the purchase of Sanjeev Kapoor books by sending this coupon along with payment to Popular Prakashan.
2. The offer is valid as per the mentioned date.
3. The coupons are valid only against the printed MRPs and will not work with any other special offers or promotions at the time of purchase.
4. The coupons are non-transferable and non-encashable.
5. No two vouchers can be clubbed together.
6. Each coupon is valid for one time purchase only.

Popular Prakashan Pvt. Ltd.
35-C, Pt. Madan Mohan Malaviya Marg, Tardeo,
Mumbai-400 034
E-Mail: info@popularprakashan.com
Phone: 91-22-24941656 Fax: 91-22-24945294

TERMS AND CONDITIONS FOR REDEMPTION

1. This coupon can be redeemed against the purchase of Sanjeev Kapoor books by sending this coupon along with payment to Popular Prakashan.
2. The offer is valid as per the mentioned date.
3. The coupons are valid only against the printed MRPs and will not work with any other special offers or promotions at the time of purchase.
4. The coupons are non-transferable and non-encashable.
5. No two vouchers can be clubbed together.
6. Each coupon is valid for one time purchase only.

Popular Prakashan Pvt. Ltd.
35-C, Pt. Madan Mohan Malaviya Marg, Tardeo,
Mumbai-400 034
E-Mail: info@popularprakashan.com
Phone: 91-22-24941656 Fax: 91-22-24945294

TERMS AND CONDITIONS FOR REDEMPTION

1. This coupon can be redeemed against the purchase of Sanjeev Kapoor books by sending this coupon along with payment to Popular Prakashan.
2. The offer is valid as per the mentioned date.
3. The coupons are valid only against the printed MRPs and will not work with any other special offers or promotions at the time of purchase.
4. The coupons are non-transferable and non-encashable.
5. No two vouchers can be clubbed together.
6. Each coupon is valid for one time purchase only.

Popular Prakashan Pvt. Ltd.
35-C, Pt. Madan Mohan Malaviya Marg, Tardeo,
Mumbai-400 034
E-Mail: info@popularprakashan.com
Phone: 91-22-24941656 Fax: 91-22-24945294

TERMS AND CONDITIONS FOR REDEMPTION

1. This coupon can be redeemed against the purchase of Sanjeev Kapoor books by sending this coupon along with payment to Popular Prakashan.
2. The offer is valid as per the mentioned date.
3. The coupons are valid only against the printed MRPs and will not work with any other special offers or promotions at the time of purchase.
4. The coupons are non-transferable and non-encashable.
5. No two vouchers can be clubbed together.
6. Each coupon is valid for one time purchase only.

Popular Prakashan Pvt. Ltd.
35-C, Pt. Madan Mohan Malaviya Marg, Tardeo,
Mumbai-400 034
E-Mail: info@popularprakashan.com
Phone: 91-22-24941656 Fax: 91-22-24945294